SEATTLE'S
LAKES, BAYS & WATERWAYS
AFOOT & AFLOAT

Including the Eastside

SEATTLE'S
LAKES, BAYS & WATERWAYS

Including the Eastside

Marge & Ted Mueller

THE
MOUNTAINEERS

Published by
The Mountaineers
1001 SW Klickitat Way, Suite 201
Seattle, WA 98134

First edition, 1998

Published simultaneously in Great Britain by Cordee, 3a DeMontfort Street, Leicester, England, LE1 7HD

Manufactured in the United States of America

Edited by Paula Thurman
Maps by Gray Mouse Graphics
All photographs © Marge and Ted Mueller
Cover design by Watson Graphics and Gray Mouse Graphics
Book design and layout by Gray Mouse Graphics

Cover photographs: *A sailing class gathers in the Washington Park Arboretum;* insets: *Kayaks explore Yarrow Bay; bicycling on the Sammamish River Trail near Bothell.*
Frontispiece: *Boats in the Montlake Cut during Opening Day of the yachting season.*

Library of Congress Cataloging-in-Publication Data

Mueller, Marge.
    Seattle's lakes, bays & waterways, afoot & afloat / Marge & Ted
Mueller. —1st ed.
       p. c.
    Includes bibliographical references (p.   ) and index.
    ISBN 0-89886-553-0
    1. Seattle Region (Wash.)—Guidebooks. 2. Lakes—Washington
(State)—Seattle Region—Guidebooks. 3. Bays—Washington (State)—
Seattle Region—Guidebooks. 4. Waterways—Washington (State)—
Seattle Region—Guidebooks. 5. Outdoor recreation—Washington
(State)—Seattle Region—Guidebooks. I. Mueller, Ted II. Title.
F899.S43M84 1998
917.96'770443—dc21   98-12172
    CIP

CONTENTS

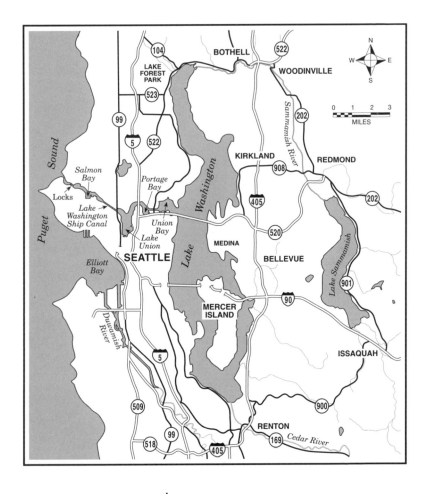

PREFACE

We originally planned the *Afoot and Afloat* books as recreation guides to all the protected marine waters of Washington. However, thinking back to long, brisk sails on Lake Washington, Fourth of July nights spent awed by fireworks on Lake Union, and fascinating walks with our children on Foster Island, we realized that urban freshwater offers as much in the way of great recreation as does saltwater. And it is close at hand—a distinct advantage to people who might not have the time, inclination, or conveyance to reach remote saltwater sites. Thus, we decided to write this, our fifth *Afoot and Afloat* guide, on the linked lakes, bays, and waterways of Seattle and the many nearby cities and towns.

A paddler enjoys the quiet water of the Sammamish River at Marymoor Park.

Boaters, paddlers, and shoreside adventurers can explore this network of channels all the way from the government locks at Salmon Bay to distant Lake Sammamish (with a few caveats to boaters in regard to the height of a mast or superstructure and a vessel's draft). These waterways beckon skippers of sailboats and power cruisers, and also paddlers in canoes, kayaks, rowboats, and inflatables.

The urban shorelines are edged by a startling amount of public property—not only large popular state, county, and city parks, but also boat launches and a wealth of miniparks. These latter public accesses, which are extended street ends converted into attractive neighborhood nooks with a bench or two and an occasional picnic table, offer the opportunity to splash your feet in the water and soak up the water's edge ambiance. Because of railroads that once ran along the shores, and thanks to insightful people who saw the recreational potential of abandoned railbeds, this area now has the combined Burke-Gilman and Sammamish River Trails—a 27-mile-long grand promenade that is the finest such route in the nation, and perhaps in the world.

In addition to the obvious developed parks, undeveloped public-owned waterfront (most notably platted street ends and waterways) is legally open to everyone. In some cases these street ends are unreachable because of brambled banks or they appear to be part of adjoining property. By publicizing these public areas, whether they are marked as such or not, we hope to make you aware of them and motivate neighborhood associations and local government agencies to properly identify them and make them fully accessible and user-friendly.

The locations described in this book were surveyed in 1997 and were double-checked with the appropriate public agencies. In a few cases we were told of soon-to-occur improvements, which we included in the text. In describing these scheduled improvements we relied on agency plans; however, plans might have changed since the manuscript was written, or there might have been delays, making the information no longer completely accurate. We would appreciate knowing about any inaccuracies, changes, or omissions. Please address any comments to us in care of The Mountaineers Books, 1001 SW Klickitat Way, Suite 201, Seattle, WA 98134, or e-mail to grmouse@aol.com.

Marge and Ted Mueller
April 1998

ACKNOWLEDGMENTS

We would like to thank the many people who were helpful in providing facts and verifying information about the public parks and shoreline property included in this book. Among these are members of the Washington Water Trails Urban Water Trail Committee, particularly its chairperson, Vivian MacKay, and its Eastside representative, Roger Johnston.

In Seattle we received assistance from Terry Dunning, Rodney Young, Mike Usen, Linda Hammond, and Rick Nishi, Seattle Parks and Recreation Department; Joe Taskey, Seattle Engineering Department; Scott Cline, Seattle City Archivist; and Sergeant Terry Jackson, Seattle Harbor Patrol.

For county parks we were helped by Shelly Farr and Stephen Johnson, King County Department of Parks and Recreation. Parks information in other local communities was provided by Gary Feroglia, Mercer Island Parks and Recreation; Roy Lehner, Redmond Parks and Recreation; Lane Youngblood, Woodinville Parks and Recreation; Mark Connley, Kirkland Parks and Community Services; Cathy Wiederhold, City of Bellevue Parks and Community Services; and Leslie Betlach, Renton Parks and Community Services.

Other persons who have been helpful are Jim Thomas, Aquatic Lands Division, Washington Department of Natural Resources; and Douglas Jennings, Capital Projects Office, University of Washington.

INTRODUCTION

A BRIEF HISTORY OF INLAND WATERWAYS

If you had been around in the late 1800s to paddle a canoe or pilot a steamboat on the waters described in this book, you would have found them significantly different from what you see today. These interlinked bodies were profoundly changed by a single event—the building of the Hiram M. Chittenden Locks.

When settlers arrived in the Puget Sound region, the water level of Lake Washington was nine feet higher than it is today. The lake shore was well upland from where it now lies, and today's marshes at Mercer Slough, Juanita Bay, and Union Bay were shallow arms of the lake. Many of today's familiar landmarks—Renton Airport, Husky Stadium, Matthews Beach Park—were under water. At the north end of Lake Washington the lake curved farther east, and part of what is now Kenmore was inundated. The Sammamish River (then called the Squak River) was much broader and deeper, making it navigable all the way to Lake Sammamish by shallow-draft steamboats.

At its south end, Lake Washington also was markedly different. The peninsula of Seward Park was an island linked to the mainland by marshes, and Pritchard Island (Atlantic City Park), unlike today, actually was an island. Wetmore Slough threaded through today's Genesee Park as a narrow channel that reached inland to Columbia City. The lake's outlet was the Black River at its south end; this drainage flowed into the Cedar River, then converged with the White River to form the Duwamish River, which drained into Elliott Bay mudflats.

When water was high in the lake, a small stream at its northwest side trickled from Union Bay across a 1/2-mile-wide isthmus into Portage Bay, an arm of Lake Union. Water draining from Lake Union flowed west via shallow Ross Creek at its northwest corner and drained into Salmon Bay.

In early days Union Bay Marsh, near the University of Washington, was under nine feet of water.

Seattle pioneers initially attempted to dig the Montlake Cut with manual labor.

This bay, which became a mudflat at minus tides, was much narrower and shallower than it is today.

As the region became settled, small communities sprung up along the lake shores—Fremont, Wallingford, Latona, Brooklyn (today's University District), and Ross (on the south side of Ross Creek, opposite Fremont). Many of these towns had water-dependent businesses such as sawmills and shipyards. Since earliest times it had been assumed that Lake Washington and Lake Union would eventually be linked—in fact, Lake Union was so named because of the planned connection. Early attempts to join the lakes were mostly token—one man attempted to dig through the Montlake isthmus with a pick and shovel. In 1885 a shallow, 16-foot-wide channel, dug with Chinese labor, was completed at that site. The canal's crude wooden locks took a beating from log rafts, so a parallel log raceway was later constructed. Ross Creek, between Lake Union and Salmon Bay, was dredged to handle small boats.

At the end of the Civil War the U.S. War Department sought to locate a naval station north of San Francisco. Lake Washington was a serious contender, and possible water connections from Puget Sound were surveyed. The Navy's interest in Lake Washington ended when Port Orchard, on the west side of the Sound, was chosen. At about this same time the Great Seattle Fire of 1889 devastated industries on Elliott Bay, and many of the sawmills relocated to Lake Union and Salmon Bay. Those on Lake Union shipped their lumber to Elliott Bay via rail, while mills on Salmon Bay had to wait for high tide to move their barge loads. Although the Navy was no longer interested in a canal, these mills, along with other industries here and newly developing ones on the northeast shore of Lake Washington at Kirkland and Bothell, continued to push for a freshwater connection to saltwater shipping.

Over the years numerous routes for the "ditch"—as it was called by its detractors—had been put forth. One was to the south, via the lake's natural outlet, following the Black, Cedar, and Duwamish Rivers, a route of some 14 miles (and bypassing Lake Union). A canal was also considered running from the south end of Lake Washington at Wetmore Cove, cutting through Rainier Valley and Beacon Hill and linking to the mouth of the Duwamish River. With private funding, this channel was actually begun in 1895. Digging proceeded from west to east across the Duwamish tideflats; however reality set in when Beacon Hill was reached in 1902 and unanticipated engineering problems developed. Faced with dwindling funds, the project was abandoned, leaving the ravine on the west side of Beacon Hill, where the I-5 freeway now exits to Columbian Way.

Three plans for a ship canal involved breaching the Montlake isthmus and utilizing Lake Union, although the final leg of their routes differed: (1) from the south end of Lake Union around the southeast side of Queen Anne Hill to Elliott Bay; (2) following Lake Union's natural outlet through Salmon Bay, then cutting south between Queen Anne Hill and Magnolia Bluff to Smith Cove on Elliott Bay; or (3) through Salmon Bay, past Ballard to Shilshole Bay. Eventually the 5-mile-long cut through Salmon Bay to Shilshole Bay won out. This route had been encouraged by Seattle entrepreneurs, Thomas Burke, John J. McGilvra, and Daniel Gilman, who (coincidentally) had heavily invested in property along the route.

Different designs for the locks were drawn up (at one point wooden structures were considered). A design by Seattle District Engineer Major Hiram M. Chittenden that employed concrete locks was selected, and in 1908 the Lake Washington Ship Canal project was approved. In order to negotiate the 35-foot differential between Lake Washington and low tide on the sound, two locks were initially planned, the major one at the Montlake Cut, and a second one at the present location. However, it was

Boats enter the large lock at Hiram M. Chittenden Locks.

determined that costs could be trimmed by eliminating the Montlake set and instead lowering the level of Lake Washington. This would cut off the Black River and reduce flood problems in the Duwamish valley.

The concrete lock walls were poured in early 1913; in July 1916 the gates were closed and the water in Salmon Bay was raised 21 feet above the high tide level. A few months later the Montlake Cut was completed between Portage and Union Bays, lowering Lake Washington 9 feet. A grand boat parade was held when the locks were officially dedicated on July 4, 1917, and people who gathered on shore cheered and threw flowers into the newly opened canal. At the time, this was the largest such facility in the Western Hemisphere except for the Panama Canal, which had been completed only three years earlier. In their first year of operation they served over 20,000 vessels. Today over 100,000 boats use it annually.

Using the Lakes, Bays, and Waterways

Public and Private Shorelands

Going hand in hand with using water is using the land that edges it. Although a good portion of shorelands are private, a heartening amount still remains public. Knowing who has jurisdiction over public lands helps you know what to expect there and what public usage is permitted.

City, county, and state parks. Well-developed facilities at city, county, and state parks usually feature picnic tables and shelters, children's play equipment, sports areas, and rest rooms, and often include swimming beaches with summer lifeguards. Some have boat launches; in a few cases moorage is available.

Many of the major parks on Lake Washington outside Seattle were purchased or developed by King County. As new local governments such as Mercer Island, Medina, and Redmond came into existence, the county transferred much of its park property to local jurisdiction. Where the authors were able to determine it, the jurisdiction for specific public property included in this book is shown in parentheses following the location name.

Street ends and miniparks. Public street ends offer a chance to reach the water for views or a quiet retreat. Aside from an occasional bench, they have no improvements. The exceptions are some street ends where neighborhood groups have worked with the city to create pleasant, well-maintained little miniparks with nice landscaping and sometimes even floats offshore. In some, additional land was acquired to enlarge the park.

Platted shoreline street ends are public unless they have been leased or deeded to individuals or permits have been issued for their use. A check of land-use records is sometimes needed to determine the status of a street end; even then records are not always current or accurate. Marking on public street ends is very spotty. In Seattle, the city is working on a new database of these lands and is attempting to verify them and mark them. Although all public street ends are *legally* open to use both by land and by water, some terminate at a high slippery bank, a thick knot of blackberry bushes, or other obstructions, making access impossible. In a few cases neighboring property owners actively work to disguise the fact that a street end is public.

The public portion of the shoreline is only the width of the street end— generally 60 to 100 feet wide. If using public street ends, park legally and respect the privacy and rights of adjoining property owners. With a considerate public, perhaps more will become developed.

Submerged shorelands. Although boaters like to think of all water as theirs to use, that is not quite true; ownership of shorelands determines whether the water above it is open to the public. Shorelands are defined as property lying between a line of ordinary high water and the line of navigability.

Washington State originally owned all tidelands, bedlands, and navigable submerged shorelands in the state, with their management vested in the Department of Natural Resources (DNR). Until the early 1970s these lands were frequently sold to private interests; for example, in 1907 the legislature approved the sale of aquatic lands along Lake Washington to finance the Alaska-Yukon-Pacific Exposition. By 1979, when the practice of selling shorelands was halted, only 39 percent of the state's tidelands and 70 percent of the shorelands remained in public ownership.

Waterways. A "waterway" (in a bureaucratic sense) is defined as an area platted across aquatic lands or created by a waterway district that provides access between uplands and open water, or between navigable bodies of water. Today there are only a few remaining state-owned waterways on Lake Washington, but a number still exist in Lake Union. These are public, DNR-owned properties below water; however, the shoreline itself is not necessarily public-owned. Thus, there can be no construction over these waterways, but the public is not guaranteed land access to them.

RECREATION—HAVE FUN, BUT WATCH THE RULES

Boating and Operating Personal Watercraft

With the greatest per-capita ratio of boats to people than any other place in the world, Seattle is well justified in calling itself the boating capital. Although much of the boating activity is on saltwater, inland waters also have endless attractions. Boats ranging from outboards to yachts can take a day's cruise on 19½-mile-long Lake Washington or stop overnight in one of the public moorage facilities or protected anchorages. Several yacht clubs have moorages and shoreside clubhouses. Boat rental or charter operations on the lakes cater to boating have-nots. For better or worse,

Seattle's Bridges

Seven bridges, both high and low, cross the Lake Washington Ship Canal, tying the two sections of Seattle together. These spans add a slight scheduling challenge, if not a navigating one, for boats traveling the channel from Puget Sound to Lake Washington. Two are high, fixed structures; the four drawbridges are opened for vessels that exceed their clearance. A railroad bridge near the west end of the locks is open except when trains are crossing it.

Clearances for each bridge are posted; however the actual clearance varies slightly because the level of the lake varies by about 2 feet from summer to winter. In the case of the railroad bridge, the tide level changes, of course. Listed from west to east, the posted vertical clearance of each bridge, measuring from the water to the center of the span, is as follows:

- Railroad bridge on west end of locks: 43 feet
- Ballard Bridge: 45 feet
- Fremont Bridge: 30 feet
- Aurora Avenue (George Washington) Bridge: 73 feet (fixed)
- Lake Washington Ship Canal Bridge (I-5 Freeway): 127 feet (fixed)
- University Bridge: 44 feet
- Montlake Bridge: 46 feet

The signal for opening a bridge for boats is one long and one short horn blast. The bridge tender will return this signal to indicate it will be raised or will sound four or more short blasts to indicate a delay. Delays might occur because of time-of-day constraints, emergency vehicle traffic, vehicular traffic build-up from a recent opening, or because the bridge tender wants to group other approaching boats for a single opening. Bridges are opened most times on request; however, from 12:30 P.M. to 3:40 P.M. they are open only on the half-hour and hour for recreational vessels, and they do not open on weekdays during the commuting hours of 7:00 A.M. to 9:00 A.M. and 3:40 P.M. to 6:00 P.M. The bridges will not open for boats under sail.

Bridges are not regularly staffed at night between 11:00 P.M. and 7:00 A.M. Vessels needing openings during that time must contact bridge operations by telephone at (206) 386-4251 or on marine VHF channel 13; a bridge tender will be dispatched. The radio channel may also be used if it is necessary to contact the bridge tender during other hours as well, but it should not be used to request routine openings.

On Lake Washington, the Evergreen Point Floating Bridge has a center drawspan. Boats needing to open it must phone 24 hours in advance to (206) 764-4100. Older charts might show a drawspan on the Mercer Island Floating Bridge; however, it is no longer there because of the traffic problems it caused. Vertical clearances on the elevated parts of the bridges are as follows:

- Evergreen Point (Albert D. Rosellini Memorial) Bridge (Highway 520): east end, 57 feet; west end, 44 feet
- Mercer Island Floating (Lacey B. Murrow and Homer M. Hadley) Bridge (I-90): east end, 71 feet; west end, 35 feet
- East Channel Bridge: 38 feet

The Fremont Bridge opens wide for a sailboat.

motorized waterbikes known as personal watercraft (PWCs) are experiencing great popularity throughout the area. The usual safety caveats regarding U.S. Coast Guard-required personal flotation devices, warning sound devices, fire extinguishers, running lights, and so forth apply to the lakes and channels as well as they do to the open waters of Puget Sound. Remember, if something goes wrong in the middle of Lake Washington, it's over 150 feet to the bottom!

Speed limits and restrictions for boats and PWCs. Coast Guard regulations apply to all waters. Most of the waterways have no speed regulations in open water. The following restrictions apply:

- In the Lake Washington Ship Canal from Shilshole Bay to Webster Point a 7-knot, no-wake speed limit is strictly enforced.
- On Lake Union within 200 yards of shore the speed limit is 7 knots.
- On Lake Washington within 100 yards of shore, docks, bridges, or other fixed objects the speed limit is 7 knots. White can buoys with horizontal red stripes placed along the Lake Washington shoreline mark the 100-yard limit.
- Under Lake Washington's floating bridges and within 100 yards of them the speed limit is 8 knots.
- The Sammamish River has a 5-mph speed limit for its entire length.
- At the entrance to the Mercer Slough the speed limit is 8 mph; in the slough, motorized craft are not permitted north of the Sweyolocken launch ramp.
- In traffic channels such as the Lake Washington Ship Canal keep to the starboard side of the channel.
- Sailboats do not have the right of way in the Lake Washington Ship Canal.

Seaplanes. Seaplanes land on and take off from open areas of Lake Washington and Lake Sammamish, the tight confines of Lake Union, and the even tighter confines of Portage Bay. In all these areas seaplanes must yield to vessels of any size. The exception is at the designated seaplane landing area on the northeast end of Lake Washington between the mouth of the Sammamish River and Arrowhead Point, which is marked by a north–south line of buoys. The boating speed limit here is 5 mph, and *within this area seaplanes have the legal right-of-way over watercraft.*

Weather. Although the inland waters of the Seattle area are somewhat protected, storms should not be lightly dismissed. Winds on Lake Washington sometimes reach 60 mph or more, and with 10 miles of fetch they can raise dangerous whitecaps. Even at lesser wind velocities, waves reflected off the windward side of the floating bridges can create stomach-wrenching chop. Conversely, the bridges can be an advantage, as their lee sides offer some protection in calmer water during high winds.

Although Lake Union and Lake Sammamish are not as long as Lake

Sailboats race on the open expanses of Lake Washington.

Washington, their north–south orientation aligns with the prevailing direction of storm winds, and hills on the sides of both lakes act as funnels that tend to increase wind velocity.

In spring and fall, early morning fog sometimes settles over the lakes, although often it is high enough above water level that it doesn't pose a navigational problem. Usually any fog burns off by mid-morning.

Hazards. Aside from stormy weather, the greatest hazard on the waterways is probably inexperienced, inconsiderate, or boozed-up boaters—avoid being one of them. In metropolitan areas such as Lake Union and the Lake Washington Ship Canal, surrounding lights on shore and reflecting off the water make it difficult to see the navigational lights of other boats. Adding to the hazard are the number of small boats such as kayaks that might be on the water at night. Be watchful.

Union Bay has only 3 to 10 feet of water outside the dredged ship canal, so deep-draft vessels need to keep a sharp eye on the depth sounder in the north portion of the bay. The north end of Lake Washington is quite shallow and has a number of pilings from old lumber mill docks and booms that have rotted off at the surface or slightly below, so caution and slow speeds are advisable in the vicinity. Several old log booms lie along the east shore of Lake Washington between Kennydale and Newcastle Parks.

Motorized craft should not attempt to run the section of the Sammamish River off the middle of Marymoor Park where a below-surface weir has only a foot or so of water clearance over the top. The mouth of the Sammamish River is quite shoal and, although there has been some dredging in the main channel used by the air harbor and adjacent marinas, it has not been extended into the mouth of the Sammamish River. Several bridges over the Sammamish River have a maximum vertical clearance of 10 to 12 feet.

Water-skiing

The long stretches of open water in Lake Washington and Lake Sammamish are favorite areas for water-skiing. On these lakes the following regulations apply:

- Water-skiing is permitted only during daylight hours.
- Water-skiing is prohibited within 100 yards of any shoreline, pier, or shore installation unless starting from or returning to shore.
- Any start from or return to shore must be made at a right angle to the shore until the 100-yard limit is reached.
- Boats towing skiers must have two persons aboard, one operator over 14 years old and one person at least 10 years old watching the skier.
- Skiers must wear an approved personal flotation device.
- Whenever a water skier is down in the water the towboat must display a 1-foot-square red flag on a 2-foot shaft.

Water-skiing is not allowed on the Lake Washington Ship Canal or the Sammamish River. On Salmon Bay, Lake Union, and Portage Bay it is prohibited within 200 yards of any shoreline, pier, or shore installation. On Union Bay between the Montlake Bridge and Webster Point water-skiers must stay at least 200 yards from the ship canal.

Paddling

Vessels of many types have plied the freshwater channels of the Seattle area for nearly 100 years. For the past 30 years powerboats and sailboats have held sway, but in recent years increasing numbers of the exercise minded have returned to human-powered craft ranging from kayaks, canoes, rowboats, and inflatable rafts to sleek racing sculls. It has been speculated that today Lake Union sees the highest number of paddlers year-round of any place in the U.S.—and possibly even the world! If you don't own a small craft, rentals are available on Lake Washington, Lake Union, and on Portage and Union Bays; several commercial enterprises offer guided trips.

The Washington Water Trails Association has recently begun an effort to create an Urban Water Trail similar to the popular Cascadia Marine Trail that stretches along saltwater shores from Olympia to Canada. Many paddlecraft launch sites described in this book might at some future date be part of this water route.

Paddlers' safety concerns. In addition to the usual hazards of bad

The Arboretum has fascinating nooks and crannies for kayakers to explore

weather and irresponsible boaters, paddlers need to be aware of several other hazards.

- First—and most important—wear a life jacket whenever you are on the water.
- A kayak riding low in storm-tossed waves can be nearly invisible from the bridge of a large yacht. Be aware of the difficulty of being seen. Bright-colored clothing and kayak are good safety precautions.
- After dark, kayaks without lights disappear into water surface reflections. Have a light of some sort—preferably a flashlight attached to your deck with suction cups; a hiker's headlamp is also helpful.
- Even in times of good visibility, don't assume larger boats see you. A watchful eye is your greatest protection—look behind you as well as in front of you for approaching boats.
- Exercise caution around moorages; a paddler exploring docks at close range has little chance of being seen by a yacht leaving a slip.
- When exploring old docks and pilings watch for dangling wires; avoid getting pinned in tight quarters.
- Erratic wave patterns in narrow channels can pose a problem for kayaks and other small boats. Be aware that the concrete walls on either side of the Fremont Cut and the Montlake Cut cause wakes from passing boat traffic to rebound.

Launch Ramps, Put-Ins, and Mooring Facilities

As described here, boat launch facilities are of two types: those with concrete ramps for launching trailered boats and those that are suitable only for putting in hand-carried watercraft such as canoes, kayaks, rowboats, and sailboards.

Launch ramps. Several of the larger parks have launch ramps for trailered boats, with fees charged; a few street ends also have boat launch ramps. Ramps often have floats alongside; it is unlawful to tie a boat to a boarding float for any extended period or to anchor in the waterway for longer than the time it takes to launch, load, or unload the boat. Some public launch ramps permit the launching of PWCs, others do not; check the local park rules.

Hand-carry put-ins. In parks, hand-carried watercraft may not be launched from designated swimming areas. In Seattle city parks, watercraft of any sort (powerboats or paddlecraft) cannot be landed at, or launched from, any park shoreline except where specifically designated. This policy is currently under review—the greatest concern appears to be the use of public land for commercial profit, such as might occur if a private kayak operation were to use a park for launching tours. Public street

Kirkland's Marina Park has mooring facilities for visiting boaters.

ends are a grayer area. Although those that are maintained are under the jurisdiction of Seattle City Parks, there is no stated policy regarding the launching of hand-carried boats at street ends.

Moorage and anchoring. On the waterways covered in this book only two public facilities, Kirkland's Marina Park and Renton's Gene Coulon Memorial Park, offer overnight guest moorage. In both cases only a small number of slips are available. In all other parks, moorage is day-use only; a few offer long-term moorages. Anchoring is not permitted in Salmon Bay east of the locks or in the Lake Washington Ship Canal. In Lake Union, anchoring outside the harbor line or in any waterway or street end requires prior written permission from the Harbor Patrol. Boats may anchor in the portion of Portage Bay southeast of a line between the Seattle and Queen City Yacht Clubs.

Within the Seattle city limits, anchoring is prohibited in Lake Washington anywhere outside the harbor line without prior written permission from the Harbor Patrol. The sole exception is Andrews Bay, on the west side of Seward Park, where anchoring is allowed for up to 72 hours. Stern lines to the shore cannot be used here, and a quiet period (no generators) is enforced between 10:00 P.M. and 8:00 A.M. Within the Kirkland city limits, anchoring is permitted only off beachfront street ends. For the remainder of the lake the only anchoring restriction is that vessels 60 feet and over may anchor in one spot for a maximum of 48 hours, and they must then move at least 1 mile from their previous anchorage.

Swimming and Wading

On Lake Washington and Lake Sammamish, several city or county parks have roped-off swimming beaches; most are guarded during summer months. Some have wading areas, offshore swim floats, docks, and bathhouses. In any of these waters swimming is restricted, by ordinance, to designated, marked swimming beaches or to a distance of 50 feet from any shore or pier unless the swimmer is accompanied by watercraft.

From the locks to Lake Washington there are no formal public swimming beaches on waterways; however, a few of the street-end miniparks in these areas offer an opportunity for wading or taking a short (unguarded) plunge. In many spots the edges of lakes and bays have accumulated the debris of over 100 years of civilization. Broken glass and rusted metal can be a hazard; wearing sandals or an old pair of tennis shoes to protect your feet is a good idea. Do not dive in undesignated swimming areas.

Pollution, fortunately, is not the hazard it formerly was. A bond issue passed in 1958 created Metro; this agency, which coordinated the financing and construction of area sewer systems, succeeded in improving the quality of Lake Washington water, resulting in the clean water enjoyed today.

Fishing and Scuba Diving

Lake Washington and Lake Sammamish, as well as the connecting waterways, offer excellent fishing for a wide variety of species. Although salmon often leap enticingly in the locks, the waters 400 feet east and 400 feet west of the Chittenden Locks are closed to all fishing. It is unlawful to fish from boats between the locks and the Fremont Bridge. Some areas are catch-and-release only for some species. *Fishing in Washington,* a booklet published annually by the Washington Department of Fish and Wildlife, covers all regulations and seasons for these waters. A license is required for taking bullfrogs, but not for crayfish.

Scuba diving is prohibited in Salmon Bay, the ship canal, Lake Union, Portage Bay, and Union Bay without a prior written permit from the Harbor Patrol. On Lake Washington, no diving is permitted in the area within 100 yards of the National Oceanographic and Atmospheric Agency (NOAA) facility at Sand Point. In all other areas scuba diving is restricted to daylight hours, divers must be accompanied by watercraft, and the dive site must be marked by a dive flag.

BEING SAFE

Emergency Assistance

The overall legal authority in incorporated areas described in this book is the local police. In all unincorporated areas of King County, legal authority rests with the county sheriff; several of the small towns along the lake rely on King County to police their marine areas. All shore areas within this book are covered by the 911 emergency telephone number system, so this should be the initial contact point for emergencies or complaints. Within state parks, the park manager or ranger assumes emergency assistance responsibilities. Harbor patrols for Seattle, Mercer Island, King County, and Kirkland are responsible for policing waters within their jurisdiction. Telephone numbers for all agencies are listed in appendix A.

Marine VHF channel 16 is monitored by the Coast Guard and the Harbor Patrol units and is the most reliable means of contact in cases of emergencies on the water. In most cases, Harbor Patrol units will respond to marine emergencies within their capabilities, regardless of jurisdiction. Nonemergency contacts should be directed to the proper authority. Citizens Band channel 9 might be monitored by the Coast Guard, but there is no commitment for a continuous radio watch on this channel.

With the growing use of cellular telephones, the cellular providers in the Puget Sound area provide a quick-dial number, *CG, that immediately connects the caller to the Coast Guard Vessel Traffic Service Center in Seattle. This center coordinates all marine safety and rescue activities for the region.

A Note About Safety

Boating, paddling, swimming, and other water and beach recreation entail unavoidable risks that every recreationist assumes and must be aware of and respect. No guidebook can alert you to every hazard or anticipate the limitations of every reader. Therefore, the descriptions of roads, trails, routes, waterways, and natural features in this book are not representations that a particular place or excursion will be safe for your party. When you follow any of the routes described in this book, you assume responsibility for your own safety.

Areas described here vary greatly in the amount and kind of preparation needed to enjoy them safely. Some might have changed since this book was written, conditions might have deteriorated, and their public access status might have been modified by purchases, leases, or usage permits. Weather conditions can change daily, or even hourly, and will affect the safety of using these waterways. An area that is safe in good weather might be completely unsafe during inclement weather.

You can meet these and other risks safely by exercising your own independent judgment and common sense. Be aware of your own limitations, those of your craft, and of conditions when or where you are traveling. If conditions are dangerous, or if you are not prepared to deal with them safely, change your plans. Because many of the lands in this book are subject to development and/or change of ownership, conditions might have changed since this book was written, making your use of some of the routes or areas unwise. Always check for current conditions, obey posted private property signs, and avoid confrontations with property owners or managers. Each year thousands of people enjoy safe recreational experiences on the inland lakes and waterways of the Seattle area. With proper preparation and good judgment, you can too.

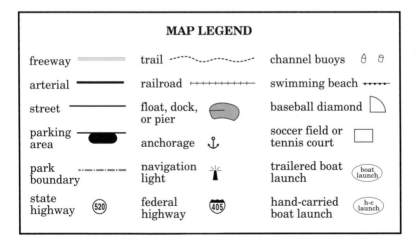

CHAPTER ONE

THE LOCKS TO LAKE WASHINGTON

The Hiram M. Chittenden Locks mark the eastern gateway to the Lake Washington Ship Canal, a freshwater channel that runs east to west, traversing the heart of Seattle. On its 8-mile-long route to the waters of Lake Washington the ship canal runs through Salmon Bay and the Fremont Cut and skirts the north edges of Lake Union and Portage Bay. After squeezing through the Montlake Cut, it crosses Union Bay to finally meet the long reaches of the lake. Along this busy urban hallway, fascinating glimpses of the city range from moldering docks, bustling marine businesses, chic houseboat communities, and tourist-oriented restaurants and shops to the University of Washington's hallowed halls (and probably even more hallowed football stadium). Stirred in with this eclectic mix are a multitude of parks, miniparks, street ends, and other public accesses where land-bound people can reach the water for an hour's or a day's recreation.

SALMON BAY AND THE LAKE WASHINGTON SHIP CANAL

Before the construction of the locks and adjoining spillway dam, Salmon Bay, the waterway between the locks and the Ballard Bridge, was a shallow salty backwater off Puget Sound. The opening of the locks in 1917 transformed the bay's water from salt to fresh, and damming and dredging deepened it enough to accommodate ships instead of just shallow-draft vessels. Shores of the bay offer a fascinating kaleidoscope of salty moorages, fancy marinas, piers piled with crab pots, tarmacs with hauled-out boats, posh restaurants, a Coast Guard buoy-tender station, and the largest fishing fleet moorage on the West Coast. A homey

Houseboat docks and private boat moorages edge Portage Bay near the Montlake Cut.

touch is added by an occasional live-aboard boat, with a tattered lawn chair, a potted evergreen, and a row of bright geraniums on deck.

Paddlers and other small craft will find the bay generally calm and well-protected from weather, but the chop generated by heavy traffic, especially when boats rush from the locks, can sometimes cause concern. Larger boats need to watch channel markers; much of the bay ranges from 15 feet deep around the docks to 30 feet deep in the channel; however, shallow areas where boats can run aground do exist—and there's no tide to float you off here! The current in the channel, which normally is at its weakest from July through December, rarely exceeds 2 knots; spring snowmelt in the mountains or heavy rains can cause it to reach 3 knots. It is strongest in narrow passages such as the Fremont and Montlake Cuts.

East of the Ballard Bridge, the ship canal funnels into a 100-foot-wide passageway. This outlet from Lake Union—originally Ross Creek—had a

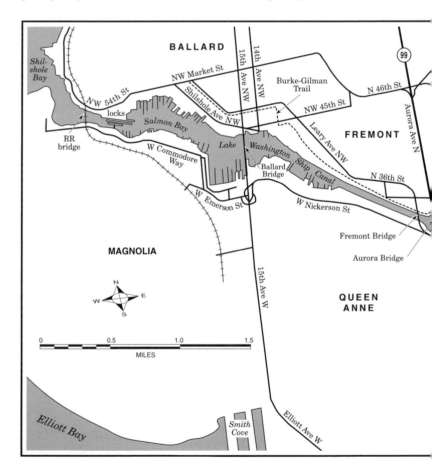

Crabbing boats and stacks of crab pots in the Lake Washington Ship Canal

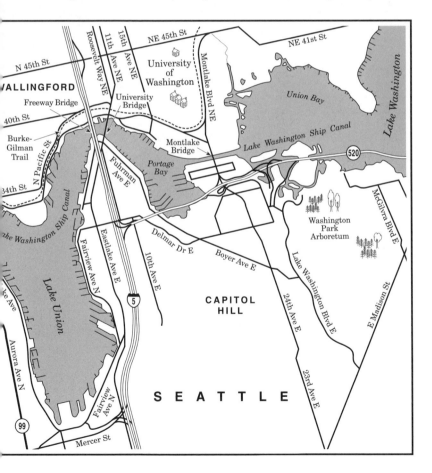

less than glamorous start. In 1884 Chinese laborers working for a local company excavated the shallow creek enough to float logs from Lake Union to Salmon Bay. In the early 1900s the U.S. Army Corps of Engineers undertook some dredging as a part of early canal-building efforts. In 1904, in order to solve a well pollution and sewage problem, three sewer drains were opened into the channel, turning it into little more than an open sewer. Today, storm drain overflow outlets can be seen along the sides of the canal. Dredging resumed in 1911, and after six years' work the canal and locks were officially opened as Seattle's premier marine thoroughfare.

As the Fremont Cut is neared, tightly packed businesses give way to concrete bulkheads, topped by a row of stately poplars, that frame the canal. The Fremont Bridge, the lowest and most frequently opened of the bascule bridges across the canal, guards the east end of this section.

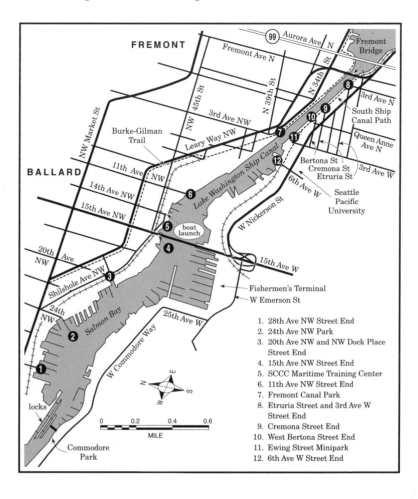

1. 28th Ave NW Street End
2. 24th Ave NW Park
3. 20th Ave NW and NW Dock Place Street End
4. 15th Ave NW Street End
5. SCCC Maritime Training Center
6. 11th Ave NW Street End
7. Fremont Canal Park
8. Etruria Street and 3rd Ave W Street End
9. Cremona Street End
10. West Bertona Street End
11. Ewing Street Minipark
12. 6th Ave W Street End

Hiram M. Chittenden Locks (U.S. Army Corps of Engineers)

Access: Land, water
Facilities: Boat locks, rest rooms, museum, gift shop, botanical gardens, fish ladder, *disabled access*

As if transporting boats between tide-influenced saltwater and the stable level of the inland waters isn't enough, the locks also serves as one of the best tourist attractions in town. Over 100,000 tugs, barges, fishing boats, tour boats, military vessels, and recreational craft squeeze through this busy gateway every year, and over a million people come to watch them. There are locks larger than these, but none in the U.S. handle more vessel traffic.

The lock complex consists of two parallel locks: the larger 825 feet long by 80 feet wide, and the smaller 150 feet long by 28 feet wide. Either can lift boats up to 26 feet, depending on the level of the tide. The locks are in operation continuously; the best boat watching is on sunny weekends. People arriving at the locks by boat are not permitted to leave their vessels to go ashore, and those on shore may not board boats.

By land, the locks are southwest of Seattle's Ballard district at the point where the Northwest Market Street arterial curves and becomes Northwest 54th Street. The large parking area at the entrance is usually crowded in summer; additional parking is on nearby streets. Walkways and viewing areas of the locks are easily negotiated by disabled persons; two disabled parking spots are inside the entrance gate.

The Carl S. English Jr. Ornamental Gardens, a beautifully landscaped 7-acre arboretum, enhances the entrance to the grounds. A tiered lawn edging the locks is the perfect spot for watching boat traffic, sunbathing, and perhaps enjoying a picnic. A visitor center, which features displays on the history and operation of the locks, is open

A tugboat enters the small lock.

11:00 A.M. to 5:00 P.M., Thursday through Monday; guided walks are conducted on weekends at 2:00 P.M.

Going through the locks can be either an adventure or an agony, depending on your frame of mind. Midweek is less chaotic than weekends, so that is a good time for your first experience. Passage time is about 25 minutes for the large lock and 10 minutes for the small one, but that doesn't count waiting time. Boats such as kayaks and canoes are permitted to use the locks; they are not required to have long lock lines, as they usually raft off other boats, where they can hang on or tie up to short mooring lines.

The procedures for locking are fully described in *Middle Puget Sound, Afoot and Afloat,* a companion volume to this book. A brochure, *Guidelines for Boaters,* available from the U.S. Army Corps of Engineers, has information on negotiating the locks. The lockmaster also holds classes that teach boaters how to lock through; further information is available on the Internet at the lock's home page (see appendix A).

A spillway dam adjacent to the small lock controls the water level of Lake Washington and the ship canal. On the south side of the dam is a fish ladder that assists salmon and seagoing trout in reaching freshwater spawning grounds. Windows permit views into the ladder's gradual steps, or weirs. Best viewing is from June through February when first salmon, then steelhead and cutthroat trout, are running. The viewing gallery can be reached from the grounds of the locks by crossing the lock gates and the walkway by the dam or from adjoining Commodore Park where there is disabled access.

24th Avenue NW Park (City of Seattle)

Access: Land, water
Facilities: Public dock

Drop in your kayak here, or tie up your boat to visit the heart of Ballard. This once-collapsed and moldering dock on the north side of the Lake Washington Ship Canal east of the locks has been reconstructed by the volunteer Ballard Neighborhood Coalition, with a grant from the Northwest Marine Trades Association. The sturdy 300-foot-long dock lies off Northwest Market Street, at the end of 24th Avenue NW between a marine repair company and a restaurant.

Boaters can make short-term stops; Ballard's interesting Scandinavian shops, restaurants, and historic sites are just a few block's stroll away. Dock-end views of Salmon Bay and the surrounding boatyards are rewarding, as are the antics of waterfowl paddling by, but fishing is not recommended due to industrial pollution. Parking might be difficult during the week, as streetside parking is mostly filled weekdays by workers in nearby shipyards. Don't park in the adjoining restaurant lot.

Fishermen's Terminal (Port of Seattle)

Access: Land

Facilities: Restaurants, fish market, marine supplies, marine repairs (all moorage is commercial, but in the future recreational moorage might be available)

Fishermen's Terminal *is* Seattle's maritime legacy—no false salty "ambiance" here; this is the real, working, fishing fleet. The facility lies 3/4 mile east of the locks on a bay at the southwest end of the Ballard Bridge. Whether approaching by car from the north over the bridge or from the south via 15th Avenue W, you'll spot the well-marked exit for the terminal.

The docks are filled with weathered fishing boats and equally weathered fishermen mending nets and making other repairs to boats and rigging. Inner floats, which have changed little since the original terminal was dedicated in 1913, are occupied by gillnetters and trawlers; the newer outer docks hold the larger purse seiners. Renovations in 1988 added 600 feet to the large northwest dock to accommodate huge factory trawlers that joined the Alaska pollock fishing fleet. Because of a decline in the fishing fleet, the Port plans to open the moorage to other types of commercial boats such as tugs, diving boats, oil skimmers, and charter tour

Commercial fishing boats line the docks at Fishermen's Terminal.

boats. Pleasure boats might possibly be permitted to moor in the future, but the working nature of the terminal will always be maintained.

The main building has a restaurant overlooking the boating activity, a fish-and-chips bar, and a seafood market—one can hardly find a place with fresher fare! Benches around a small grass and concrete cranny just west of the main terminal are ideal for a leisurely brown bag lunch on sunny days. A striking 30-foot-high concrete pillar honors Seattle-area fishermen who have died at sea. Their names are listed on a series of plaques. The pillar is topped with a bronze sculpture of a fisherman bringing in a catch; the sculpture's bas-relief base shows marine animals ranging from salmon to octopus and crab.

Seattle Central Community College Maritime Training Center and 15th Avenue NW Street End
Access: Land

On the north side of the ship canal, east of the Ballard Bridge on Shilshole Avenue NW, is the Maritime Training Center, operated by Seattle Central Community College (SCCC). Students here learn to work on commercial vessels and in other phases of the maritime industry. The beach and picnic area on the grounds are open for public access during college operating hours. A small lagoon has a picnic table on shore and a couple more on a small dock. The remainder of the campus (including the rest rooms) are for school use only.

Unfortunately, picnics draw moochers—Canada geese often crowd the area wing-to-wing, begging for a handout. Sanitation is not one of their strong points, so bring something to cover the benches if you plan to sit down. Parking is along Shilshole Avenue NW; slots near the entrance are for school faculty.

There is no spot to put in boats on the SCCC campus, but you can reach a no-bank street end where paddlecraft can be dropped in by continuing east on Shilshole Avenue to 15th Avenue NW, which parallels the east side of the Ballard Bridge. Turn south for a short block to reach a public street end. Adjoining property under the bridge is used for parking and storage of assorted city junk. Be careful of debris at water's edge when launching.

14th Avenue NW Public Boat Launch (City of Seattle)
Access: Land, water
Facilities: Boat launch ramp, boarding float, sani-can, *disabled access*

The only public boat launch ramp between the locks and the Fremont Cut is on the north side of the ship canal, one block east of the Ballard Bridge. From Northwest 45th Street, turn south on 14th Avenue NW, and in two blocks find a two-lane concrete launch ramp with a loading pier and boarding float. The dock along the east side of the ramp is private. A gravel parking lot on the ramp's west side is big enough for a few cars or boat trailers; parking next to the ramp is reserved for disabled persons.

The Burke-Gilman Trail: Ballard to the UW
(City of Seattle)
Access: Land
Facilities: Multi-use trail, benches, *disabled access*

One of the area's greatest recreational treasures is the Burke-Gilman Trail. Nearly any time of day this blacktop path sees all manner of hikers, bikers, joggers, skaters, Rollerbladers, baby strollers, and dog walkers as well as disabled persons in both ordinary wheelchairs and ultralight sports chairs. And when Seattle receives a rare heavy snowfall, the trail even hosts cross-country skiers. The variety of ways people propel themselves along the trail is truly fascinating. Motorized conveyances are not permitted. A few benches and an occasional picnic table along the route offer spots for some R&R. Access to the trail is from any of numerous streets that edge or cross the trail. The only public rest rooms are at parks on the route; parking is at these parks or on trailside streets.

Joggers on the Burke-Gilman Trail

The trail is a hand-me-down from the railroads that once transported passengers and goods throughout the area. And what a hand-me-down it is! Sections of the abandoned railroad bed have been acquired since 1976, and the route has grown piecemeal until it now is a grand, nearly 18-mile-long route running from Seattle's Ballard district all the way to Blyth Park in Redmond. It is one of the oldest and most popular such rail-trails in the U.S.

Currently, the trail's west end follows the old railroad right-of-way to 11th Avenue NW. From there it departs from the right-of-way and follows 11th for three blocks to Leary Way NW, then continues for another 3/4 mile, ending at Northwest Market Street. In the future it might follow the railbed from 11th Avenue all the way to Golden Gardens, adding some 3 1/2 scenic miles to its length.

Heading east from 11th Avenue NW, the flat, paved path follows the railroad right-of-way to North Canal Street, from there it edges the ship canal, passes the Fremont Bridge, and goes under the Aurora Bridge. Eastward from here the route moves 1/2 block upland from the water and reaches Gas Works Park 2 1/2 miles from its start. The trail now shifts uphill a short distance and offers expansive views of the north shore of Lake Union before it reaches the University Bridge and the southeast edge of the UW campus in another mile. It pulls away from the waterway as it skirts the south and east edges of the campus for 1 1/2 miles. The remainder of the route is described in chapters 3 and 4.

Fremont Canal Park (City of Seattle)

Access: Land
Facilities: Benches, deck, shelter, *disabled access*

In the Fremont Cut, midway along the ship canal, the water corridor narrows and is bordered by tree-lined concrete bulkheads before it ducks under the Fremont Bridge. A little gem of a park sits just above the canal on a block-long steel deck with a long, continuous bench. A small covered shelter that offers respite from Seattle mists is decorated with two tile murals. One mural depicts how this spot must have looked in 1875 when, instead of the canal, tiny Ross Creek flowed from Lake Union through the infant towns of Fremont, Ross, and Ballard to reach Salmon Bay.

Parking can be found next to the Burke-Gilman Trail at the corner where 2nd Avenue NW turns southeast to become North Canal Street (one-way, eastbound). Walk across the trail and follow the path to stairs and a ramp leading to the deck. Spend a quiet hour wetting a fishline or watching the Fremont Bridge go up and down. When the locks empty their load of boats, traffic is especially concentrated. At times large vessels such as NOAA research ships come through, nearly filling the cut from wall to wall.

Fremont Canal Park

South Ship Canal Path and Adjacent Miniparks
(City of Seattle)
Access: Land
Facilities: Multi-use trail, benches, viewing platform, *disabled access*

While the north side of the Lake Washington Ship Canal has its well-known Burke-Gilman Trail, the south side has its rail-trail, too, although it is not as long. Slightly less than 1 mile of the old Burlington Northern right-of-way has been paved between the Fremont Bridge and 6th Avenue W and is now the South Ship Canal Path. The old rails and ties still remain west from 6th Avenue for 1 1/2 miles to the Ballard Bridge and south from the Fremont Bridge for 1 3/4 miles to South Lake Union Park. Hopefully, the remainder of the trail eventually will be extended.

Accesses to the completed section of the trail are at street ends. The route, which follows along the bulkhead that edges the canal and skirts the Seattle Pacific University (SPU) sports fields, is paved most of the way, although in one section the pedestrian portion of the tread is gravel.

Picnic tables between Queen Anne Avenue N and the Ewing Street Minipark are often used by office workers and SPU students. The many canal-side benches testify to the joys of leisurely watching boat traffic, ranging from racing shells, kayaks, and a variety of pleasure boats to leviathan tugs and barges. Flotillas of ducks, geese, and gulls put on an alternate floor show.

Etruria Street and 3rd Avenue N Street End. From the intersection of Etruria Street and 3rd Avenue N, just west of the Fremont Bridge, a long concrete ramp descends from the street to the South Ship Canal Path. Parking in the vicinity of the intersection is limited to customers of local businesses. Wildly colored, fanciful murals decorate the concrete walls on either side of the ramp. A small grass knoll adjacent to the bridge holds a pair of benches that offer a duck's-eye view of the frequent openings of the bascule bridge.

A few hundred yards to the west, a driveway at the junction of Nickerson Street and Etruria Street leads into parking lots for waterside office buildings. The lots are private, but the walkway along this entrance is public. Park on Nickerson and walk one block to a triangular bit of grass above the path. A few trees and some park benches are scattered around the park's perimeter. It is a nice place for a leisurely lunch, a dash of sunbathing, and views of canal traffic.

Cremona Street End. This block-long section of Cremona Street ends at a flagpole and a nice set of benches. The street end, which runs between two office buildings, butts into the South Ship Canal Path, where additional benches line the bulkhead. Nearby parking is reserved for the office park.

West Bertona Street End. Just east of the athletic field behind SPU's Royal Brougham Pavilion, at the intersection of West Bertona Street and Queen Anne Avenue N, a short street ends at a tiny landscaped square near the South Ship Canal Path. Park along Nickerson Street.

Bright murals decorate walls along the South Ship Canal Path.

The folks take the youngsters (twenty-four of them!) out for a paddle.

Ewing Street Minipark. Directly across the cut from the Fremont Canal Park is another water's edge minipark. The entrance is at the junction of 3rd Avenue W and West Ewing Street, near Royal Brougham Pavilion. A large parking area (two-hour limit) extends east from the street junction, between the pavilion and the water. Benches on the narrow grass strip above the canal's concrete bulkhead provide a picnic lunch site *par excellence*—attested to by the many freeloading ducks and geese who collect here, pleading that "Don't Feed the Waterfowl" signs be ignored. Picnic tables on a wooden platform that tops a Metro pumping station provide an elevated view of boat traffic.

Just outside the entrance to Ewing Minipark, at 3rd Avenue W, a tree-bordered lawn adjacent to the Metro Seattle Environmental Laboratories is also open to the public. A kiosk at the corner of the building describes the facility's field and laboratory activities. The 30-foot-long concrete float in front of the labs is used by the SPU rowing crew. Public access to the float is available, with permission from the school; call (206) 281-2922.

6th Avenue W Street End. At the west end of the South Ship Canal Path, this street end on the canal's south side offers a small place to reach the water and possibly launch hand-carried boats. The stub of 6th Avenue W just north of West Ewing Street ends in a no-bank water access between a couple of private floats. Streetside parking can be found.

Street Ends from Salmon Bay to Lake Union

A couple of street ends along the north shore of the Lake Washington Ship Canal are open for public use. Another street end that is public, although it has no upland access because of brambles, is at 20th Avenue NW and Northwest Dock Place.

28th Avenue NW. South from Northwest Market Street, 28th Avenue NW crosses an abandoned railroad track and drops in a short block to a street end between buildings and piers. The gentle bank is easily approached by land, so paddlecraft can be put in without difficulty.

11th Avenue NW. The only other marked public access on the canal's north side is at the end of 11th Avenue NW, three blocks east of the boat launch ramp. The adjoining Diver's Institute of Technology and a commercial boatyard have moored boats and a large barge in this waterway, leaving only skimpy space for public use.

LAKE UNION

The diversity of this ultimate urban lake yields an exciting, fascinating mix for those visiting, either by land or water. Houseboats, yacht brokerages, marinas, NOAA vessels, office buildings, marine repair, drydocks, shipbuilders, restaurants—all blend in the colorful potpourri of the shore. At night the lake becomes a glittering well, with lights of surrounding buildings and downtown high-rises reflecting in the water.

So much for the shoreline, but what of the lake's center? It too experiences the schizophrenia of the shoreline. Seaplanes take off and land amidst the comings and goings of sailboats, cruisers, kayaks, canoes, sailboards, PWCs, tugs towing barges, and every other type of craft imaginable. Tuesday evenings during summer this tight waterway experiences the "Duck Dodge," an impromptu, jovial sailboat race, open to all comers, in which the only rule is that if a boat forces a duck to change its paddling path, the boat must turn a complete circle before continuing.

Best time of all is Fourth of July, when the lake hosts a spectacular fireworks display, and thousands of boats anchor in the lake, while over 100,000 people watch from shore. In early December gaily decorated and lighted boats gather here in the evening and then form a festive holiday flotilla to parade along the shorelines and serenade onlookers.

The 600-acre, U-shaped lake, is roughly 1/2-mile wide by 1 1/2-miles long and its depth is fairly uniform, ranging from 35 to 50 feet. A major traffic channel runs across its north end. At this end of the lake a narrow buoy-marked shoal extends from the peninsula where Gas Works Park is located. A large shoal, also buoy marked, is at the lake's southwest end. The only source of boat fuel on the lake or ship canal is a marina on the lake's west shore, east of the Aurora Bridge. An east–west oriented speed test area in the center of the lake is marked by buoys; turns at either end are limited to 7 knots.

For paddlers, a circuit of the lake's perimeter is about 4 1/2 miles, but this depends on how many ins and outs of docks you explore (and how much you are diverted by restaurants and other attractions). The greatest hazard in this confined waterway is speeding boaters—be on the alert.

Sailing on Lake Union beneath the shadow of the Space Needle.

Early morning, before large boats and PWCs rev up their engines, is the best paddling time. Several put-ins around the lake are described here. A commercial kayak center on the west shore that sells and rents boats, as well as offering tours and lessons, permits private kayaks to be put in from their docks, providing they do not conflict with the center's activities.

Waterways No. 23, 22, 21, and 20 (DNR)

Several DNR-owned waterways lie on the north end of Lake Union. Two have nice accesses where people can reach the shore; two others are not usable from land, but can be explored by paddlecraft. The first of these, **Waterway No. 23**, was rezoned to allow the Lake Washington Rowing Club to build a float for launching club members' racing sculls. This 170-foot-wide waterway immediately east of the Aurora Bridge remains a public access, however. The float may be used by the public to put in boats, providing club use is not impeded. Nearby parking on North Northlake Way is restricted to rowing club members and customers of nearby businesses.

Waterway No. 22, at the south end of Stone Way N, marks the point where a trolley line once crossed a bridge, and then followed the lake's west shore to downtown Seattle. When the ship canal was complete and the Fremont Bridge was built, the fixed bridge was removed and the trolley ceased operating. Today a steep, 8-foot-high, brambled bank makes land access impossible, but the 169-foot-wide channel can still be explored by water.

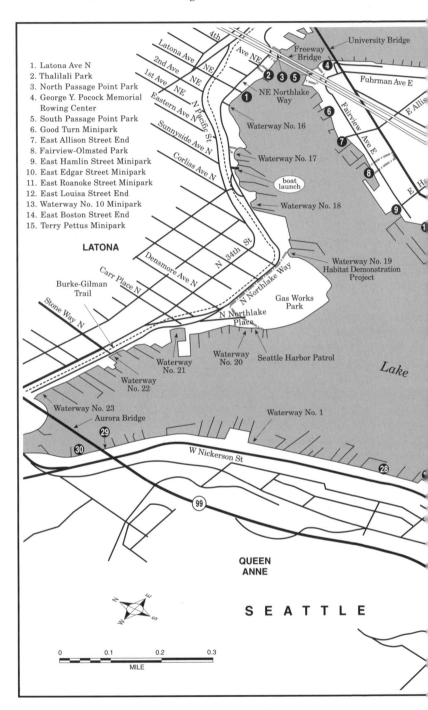

1. Latona Ave N
2. Thalilali Park
3. North Passage Point Park
4. George Y. Pocock Memorial Rowing Center
5. South Passage Point Park
6. Good Turn Minipark
7. East Allison Street End
8. Fairview-Olmsted Park
9. East Hamlin Street Minipark
10. East Edgar Street Minipark
11. East Roanoke Street Minipark
12. East Louisa Street End
13. Waterway No. 10 Minipark
14. East Boston Street End
15. Terry Pettus Minipark

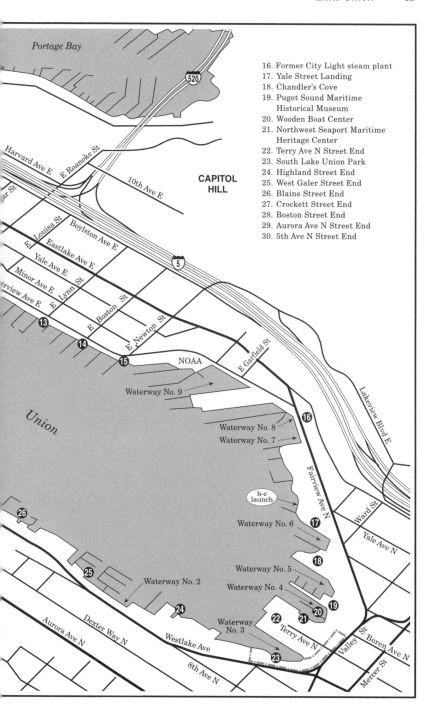

16. Former City Light steam plant
17. Yale Street Landing
18. Chandler's Cove
19. Puget Sound Maritime Historical Museum
20. Wooden Boat Center
21. Northwest Seaport Maritime Heritage Center
22. Terry Ave N Street End
23. South Lake Union Park
24. Highland Street End
25. West Galer Street End
26. Blaine Street End
27. Crockett Street End
28. Boston Street End
29. Aurora Ave N Street End
30. 5th Ave N Street End

At **Waterway No. 21**, at the intersection of North Northlake Way and Carr Place N, an adjoining shipyard improved the shore side by building a 30-foot-wide wooden deck with a planter and benches for public use. Here is a chance to view the industrial side of Lake Union, with its busy cranes, tugboats, and floating drydocks. Floats blocking the waterway prevent access from the water.

Waterway No. 20, a nondescript 120-foot-wide waterway, roughly in the vicinity of Densmore Avenue, is immediately west of the Seattle Harbor Patrol docks. There is no land access.

Gas Works Park (City of Seattle)

Park Area: 20.75 acres
Access: Land, water (shallow-draft boats)
Facilities: Picnic shelters and tables, play barn, children's play equipment, kite hill, rest rooms, benches, public art, concession stand (open in summer). *No wading, swimming, or fishing*

This, one of Seattle's premier parks, is a study in the fine craft of turning an eyesore into art and industry into recreation. The stark, rusty towers with their pipes, valves, catwalks, tanks, and smokestacks are now seen as an enormous, abstract sculpture (questionably enhanced by modern-day graffiti).

The park began in 1906 as a plant that converted coal to gas. The coal-conversion process regularly blanketed the area with smoke and soot; in 1937 the plant was converted from coal to oil. It remained in service for another 20 years, until pipelines brought natural gas to the Northwest. The city purchased the abandoned facility and in the 1970s converted it to a park. Although the towers have been fenced off for safety reasons, a large portion of the building housing the compressor equipment was retained as a children's play barn; the giant flywheels, pistons, tanks, and interconnecting piping, now painted gaudy colors, are inviting to climb on, over, and through. Picnic tables sit on a deck below the barn.

Queen Anne Hill and Capitol Hill bound the lake, forming a natural north–south funnel for winds and guaranteeing ideal conditions for flying kites. And fly kites, people do! At nearly any time of year, fanciful creations are launched from Kite Hill, a 50-foot-high mound on the park's west side. The sky above the park is often laced with box kites, tiger kites, dragon kites, Mylar monsters, and even stick- and trash-bag models.

Gas Works Park should boast one of the prime swimming beaches in the city, but unfortunately underwater sediment is so heavily polluted with toxic chemicals that wading, swimming, and fishing are prohibited; beaching paddlecraft is also prohibited here. By water, the park can be accessed via the concrete deck and bulkhead at the park's southern tip. There is no designated dock area, but small boats can tie up to the railing.

Kite Hill in Gas Works Park is good for music, too.

Passing boat traffic can make the spot quite rough, and nearby waters are shallow. A hand-carry launch is also possible at Waterway No. 19 at the park's northeast edge.

Gas Works Park is on North Northlake Way between the Fremont and University Bridges. Parking lots are on the north and west sides. Because it lies along the route of the Burke-Gilman Trail, it is a favorite stopover for cyclists and joggers using the trail.

Waterway No. 19 Habitat Demonstration Project
(City of Seattle, DNR)
Access: Land, water
Facilities: Path, hand-carried boat launch

An intriguing project to restore a microcosm of three different wildlife habitats is tucked into a water's edge street end off North Northlake Way on the east side of Gas Works Park. Here the cooperative efforts of several agencies has created a delightful miniature cove. Brightly colored, highly scented plants lure butterflies and hummingbirds, while songbirds and small mammals seek the protection of brush, shrubs, and trees growing here. Shoreline vegetation hosts waterfowl and aquatic mammals. Willow branches overhanging the beach form quiet nooks where you can watch for wildlife drawn to this unique beachfront. The shallow, graveled shore is an easy spot to put in boats that are hand-carried the short distance from the park's load/unload road loop.

The Seattle Harbor Patrol

Speeding boats, capsized canoes, partying football fans, and seagoing Santas all fall in the jurisdiction of the Seattle Harbor Patrol, an arm of the Seattle Police Department. This unit, based on Lake Union's north shore, handles all policing responsibilities on Puget Sound from West Point to the north city limits, on the waters of Salmon Bay, the ship canal, Lake Union, and the west half of Lake Washington within the city limits. The remainder of Lake Washington is handled by harbor patrols from Mercer Island, King County (primarily during summer months), and occasionally Kirkland.

The Seattle unit has three large patrol boats, ranging up to 38 feet long, as well as smaller inflatables and a Boston Whaler. The large boats have low-volume water pumps with limited fire-fighting ability; more powerful pumps are anticipated in the future. These pumps can also be used to pump water out of sinking boats—something to keep in mind. And yes, they can issue DUI citations to intoxicated skippers.

The Harbor Patrol welcomes visitors to its station on the east side of Gas Works Park, just off North Northlake Place; if their duties permit, officers will answer safety questions and conduct an informal tour. In case of emergency, the Harbor Patrol monitors VHF Channel 16 and can be contacted by phone at the number listed in appendix A.

A boat of the Seattle Harbor Patrol heads out.

Sunnyside Avenue Launch Ramp (City of Seattle)

Access: Land, water
Facilities: Boat launch ramp, boarding pier, sani-can, *disabled access*

The only public launch facility on Lake Union for trailered boats is on the north shore at the intersection of North Northlake Way and Sunnyside Avenue N. A 45-foot-long wooden dock along the west side of the two-lane concrete ramp facilitates loading and unloading. Parking for cars and trailers is on the north side of North Northlake Way. If launching a sail-boat, check the mast height as there are overhead powerlines at the top of the ramp.

Waterways No. 18, 17, and 16 (DNR)

At the foot of Corliss Avenue N, east of Gas Works Park, dense growth along North Northlake Way masks a small grass flat above **Waterway No. 18**, a 190-foot-wide public waterway. At its west side the brush gives way to a rough roadway leading down to water's edge. A number of boats moor at a private float along the waterway's west edge. No amenities here—just a nice shaded strip of grass with a few bushes at waterline, with easy access for paddlecraft from either land or water.

Waterway No. 17 holds a tiny park with 180 feet of beachfront at Eastern Avenue N and Northeast Northlake Way. Just west of the parking lot for a restaurant that is sometimes closed, the shore tapers down to water's edge. A path leads to a graveled park set with a few primitive benches—an ideal spot to sip an iced latté, wade, or drop in a canoe. Park along the street.

Waterway No. 16, a 186-foot-wide section of Lake Union shoreline at the south end of 2nd Avenue NE has a jumble of old docks and pilings that are currently undergoing reconstruction. There is no feasible land access, but paddlecraft can explore, with caution.

Thalilali Park (City of Seattle)

Access: Land, water
Facilities: Benches, historical displays, hand-carried boat launch

Here is not just another little neighborhood park—it is a mother lode of local history, presenting the compelling story of Lake Union and communities that edge it. Come here to enjoy the view, the beach, and a quiet lunch, and you will return to absorb more of this area's past.

At Northeast Northlake Way and 4th Avenue NE, west of Ivar's Restaurant, a path that winds down to water's edge leads past four boulder-rimmed nooks. Many of the boulders display vignettes of the area's past: photos of early Native Americans, historic boats, and the Aurora Bridge construction, as well as reproductions of community plats and old steamer tickets. A large

Thalilali Park on the north side of the ship canal

bronze compass displays a bas-relief map of the lake and surrounding communities. Native American words carved in a line of bricks, along with their English translation, tell what this lake represented to the region's original inhabitants: a source of fish and drinking water, a cleansing pool, a mystical body of water. Also inscribed here are the names of the young districts of Latona, Ravenna, and others that sprang up with the coming of the settlers.

North Passage Point Park (City of Seattle)
Park Area: 0.79 acres
Access: Land, water
Facilities: Benches, picnic tables, hand-carreied boat launch, *disabled access*

On Northeast Northlake Way, directly under the Ship Canal Bridge, a swath of grass leads to a deck at the north edge of the passage between Lake Union and Portage Bay. This spot has long served as a link between the north and south sides of Lake Union. Early pioneers paddled across the 500-foot-wide channel from the tiny community of Latona on the north shore; the low wooden bridge built here in the late 1800s was eventually replaced by the University Bridge. When the I-5 Freeway Bridge was built in 1962, this site and its companion to the south served as staging areas for the construction.

The tiny park, set off from surrounding property by a quieting line of trees and shrubs, offers a pair of picnic tables and arms-length-away views of passing boat traffic. Willows dip gracefully into the water above the shore; steps descend to a water-lapped bulkhead. The shore below the steps drops off quickly.

George Y. Pocock Memorial Rowing Center

Access: Land, water
Facilities: Docks, sculls (for member use), rowing classes, hand-carried boat launch from one dock

George Pocock was one of the world's most respected designers and builders of racing sculls. However, Pocock, who died in 1976, was not only a master boat builder but also a coach, motivator, and inspirational guide for many of the world's best scull-racing crews. The foundation named for him offers for-fee classes in rowing, ranging from beginners to rowers training for international competition; special programs include those for underprivileged youth and for the physically challenged.

The center is located at 3320 Fuhrman Avenue E, on the northeast shore of Lake Union. Huge bays in the building's lower floor are stacked full of shells for member use. The west leg of the broad Y-shaped launching float below the building, adjacent to South Passage Point Park, is open to public launching of nonmotorized boats.

East Shore Parks (City of Seattle)

Access: Land, water
Facilities: Picnic tables, benches, some parks have floats, *some parks are disabled accessible*

Thanks largely to the efforts of neighborhood groups, a number of prettily landscaped little parks along the east side of Lake Union offer a brief shoreside escape to nearby apartment dwellers as well as visitors.

South Passage Point Park. This wide grass slope, a companion to the park just across the channel on the north shore, also lies under the I-5 freeway deck. A pair of picnic tables overlook the waterway; concrete steps and a ramp for disabled access head down to a bulkhead and walkway at water's edge. A small alcove in the bulkhead offers a short, narrow section of shallow, rocky beach. Close-passing boats spark dreams of yacht ownership; reality is served by the ability to hand-launch small boats, either here or at nearby Pocock Rowing Center float.

The Houseboat Community

Although they are not a public facility, houseboats are such a part of Seattle's inland waterfront that they are looked on as a public treasure. Most are grouped on the east side of Lake Union and on the south shore of Portage Bay. The best place to see the houseboats from land is on Fairview Avenue E; water provides a "front yard" view for boaters and paddlers. These are not RV versions of boats, but bona fide houses that have gone to sea—or lake, in this case. Houseboats have been on the lake since the early 1900s, when small land-built houses were moved onto log rafts. Many of the older houseboats are still supported by logs, reinforced by large chunks of high-density Styrofoam. Modern floating homes that are built for this life are on concrete pontoons.

Early houseboats were a disreputable sort—many housed gambling dens and prostitutes. During the 1950s their low rent and funky lifestyle made them the favored housing of students and "hippies." The 1970s brought respectability. Prior to that time, sewage from the homes drained directly into the lake below. This was eventually recognized as an unsavory practice, and owners were pressured to connect to city sewers. Once their sanitary problems had been resolved, houseboats became "floating homes." With their permanence and respectability established, and with the increase in the cost of waterfront property, their value skyrocketed. Numerous homes were designed and constructed specifically as floating homes, with architecture rivaling the most posh of land residences; but many of the older houses remain, making the houseboat colony a delightfully colorful mixture of kitsch and class.

You can have good views of houseboats from streets or water. If

Good Turn Minipark (East Martin Street). A street-end waterway between the 3100 and 3200 blocks of Fairview Avenue E holds a tiny park favored by local folk and waterfowl. You might even spot beavers who have taken up residence in the lake. Landscaping and artfully laid out logs and boulders separate parking from a graveled beachfront that tapers into the lake's northeast corner. A concrete pad at the park's edge holds a picnic table. The adjoining waterfront building to the south has a deck in front of it which is also open to public use. The long bench here is a perfect spot to relax and enjoy water traffic and the sun (when it's out).

Fairview-Olmsted Park (Waterway No. 11). Fairview-Olmsted Park joins the waterfront to the busy thoroughfare of Eastlake Avenue E. From a streetside entry landing on Eastlake, an elevated staircase zigzags down you view the houseboats from the water, either by kayak or larger boats, keep a respectful distance. Remember you are, in essence, in these folks' front yards. Although in many cases houseboat owners enjoy looking at your boat as much as you enjoy seeing their homes, loud music or intrusive, obnoxious behavior is not welcome. *All houseboat docks are private.* Unless you are a guest of a houseboat owner, do not disembark from your boat onto docks, and do not walk down docks from land. Floating home tours, in which you may see the interiors of selected homes (for a fee), are available every year; they are well publicized.

Roanoke Reef moorage, seen here from East Roanoke Street Minipark, has modern houseboats on concrete pontoons.

the steep slope to a path that circles a grassy flat before joining Fairview Avenue E. Across Fairview a wooden gangway leads to a water-level float designed for ease in launching paddlecraft. Paddlers launching boats here can bring them in on Fairview; there is no nearby parking, so vehicles must be moved elsewhere after unloading. The best parking is along Eastlake.

A p-patch community garden edges the park's south side. Below it, a water's edge path holds more benches where gardeners can rest from their labors and nongardeners, content to eat grocery store tomatoes, can laze away an afternoon. The few parking spaces on the south side of the p-patch are for loading, park maintenance, and disabled vehicles.

East Hamlin Street Minipark. A formerly bramble-choked embankment

Terry Pettus Minipark is among the houseboat moorages.

has been transformed into a pleasant little park. Just off the end of East Hamlin Street, a pair of picnic tables sit on a graveled flat surrounded by low shrubbery. Two benches snuggled into the curved rock bulkhead are ideal for a romantic tryst. A timber staircase leads to the water. The beach is shallow and sandy but it has debris on the bottom; use caution when wading. The view out the narrow waterway overlooks the lake's north end and Gas Works Park. South are houseboats and moored boats.

East Roanoke Street Minipark. North of East Roanoke Street, Fairview Avenue E is interrupted for 1½ blocks by houseboats at Roanoke Reef and Mallard Cove. At the end of East Roanoke Street another minipark holds a few benches on a small, street-level flat. A second section of the park to the north of the street end, tucked behind trees, offers benches overlooking a side channel running between two rows of modern houseboats. This park does not have the gradually sloping, easy access to the water that the two little parks to the south have; a small wood float alongside an adjacent restaurant can be used as a temporary moorage if you are visiting the shore by water.

These houseboats are on the site of an over-the-water condominium project that ran afoul of zoning changes. When it failed, the present houseboat moorages were developed. Although there is no street-end beach, the extension of East Edgar Street is an open channel that provides paddlers access to the area between the two houseboat piers where the intriguing architecture of these newer floating homes can be viewed at close range.

Waterway No. 10 Minipark. This small, 120-foot-wide park, tucked between houseboat docks and a large waterfront condominium at the intersection of Fairview Avenue E and East Lynn Street, is almost a duplicate of Terry Pettus Minipark, farther south. A pair of picnic tables on a small grassy bench are hidden from the street by a cluster of low pines. A deck near water level holds benches inset into notches in a wooden bulkhead. The beach is gentle and sandy, ideal for splashing around or taking a cooling swim on a hot summer day. When the weather is not so nice, mallards abound.

Terry Pettus Minipark. This park, landscaped with pines and ivy, is at Fairview Avenue E and East Newton Street. A lone picnic table sits at street level, amid ivy. Stairs descend to water level, where there is a narrow wooden deck leading out to a float. Benches are tucked in alcoves in the bulkhead above the deck. The small float and sloping beach invite wading or swimming. The park is named for a long-time social activist who led the houseboat community in its struggle for survival in the late 1960s.

Waterways No. 9, 8, and 7 (City of Seattle and DNR)

Access: Land, water
Facilities: Picnic table, bench, waterside walkway, float

Here is still true working waterfront! **Waterway No. 9** lies on the southeast side of Lake Union at Fairview Avenue E and East Garfield, south of Terry Pettus Minipark. From the street the huge vessels of the West Coast NOAA oceanographic fleet can be seen through a fence. During Christmas season a trim of colored lights outlining the ships gives a festive touch. Paddlers can get good duck-level views of the oceanographic vessels as well as large ships undergoing maintenance and repair at the adjacent Lake Union Drydock Company; however, there is no upland access.

The former City Light steam plant is a conspicuous landmark on **Waterway No. 8.** Built in 1914, it was last used to generate electricity in 1980. The deteriorating structure was rehabilitated in 1994 and became the home for a biotechnology company. Because of the historical significance of the old plant, the company was required to preserve its architectural integrity (down to replacing the rusted old smokestacks with fiberglass look-alikes—albeit adorned with the company name).

Waterways No. 8 and 7, below the plant, at one time were moorage

space for oil barges that supplied the plant, as well as the site of the in-
take and outlet for steam plant water. The restoration package required
these waterways to become more "people friendly." As a result, the bank
where the old flumes once were now has stairs leading to a nice 200-foot-
long floating walkway. A large float near its south end provides easy put-
in and retrieval of paddlecraft. A few rotting offshore pilings from the old
fuel docks are scenic or a nuisance, depending on your point of view. A
couple of spots by a nearby restaurant are public parking, or you can park
in the restaurant lot for a fee.

South Lake Union

Access: Land, water
Facilities: Restaurants, boat rentals, shops, historical displays, yacht
brokers, tour boats, benches, picnic tables, waterfront boardwalk, hand-
carried boat launch, rest rooms, marine pumpout station

Lake Union becomes increasingly urban as it reaches its south end.
The relaxed ambiance of houseboats and tiny parks changes to bustling
businesses capitalizing on the scenic location. The view sweeps north the
length of the lake, encompassing sailboats, cruisers, seaplanes, and working ships, all capped by the distant, tangled towers of Gas Works Park. Beyond the old steam plant a path runs along the shore, ducking below
parking lots, restaurants, and yacht brokerages. Enjoy a brown bag lunch
or goodies from nearby eateries at one of the benches along the path.

Yale Avenue N Access. Wedged between a restaurant and a yacht
broker's docks at the end of Yale Avenue N you'll find a tiny sliver of public land. The ramp here drops to a small concrete float with 40 feet of
space for visiting boats. Moorage is limited to three hours. At the out-
board end of the float is one of the few marine head pumpout stations on
the lake. Hand-carried boats can be launched here, but parking might be
a problem, as most adjoining lots are for customers of adjacent businesses.

Yale Street Landing and Chandler's Cove. A wood-decked promenade
edged by planters of bright flowers wraps around two large neighboring
piers that hold shops, restaurants, yacht sales offices, and tour boat operations. Openings in the railing of the Chandlers Cove pier permit visiting
boats to tie up to visit; a float along the pier's west side is also available for
short-term tie-ups. Tour boats operating from here offer cruises of Lake
Union and Lake Washington as well as trips through the locks to the Seattle waterfront on Elliott Bay.

Floats in **Waterway No. 6** serve as brokerage showrooms for sail- and
powerboats; a sales and rental shop for canoes and kayaks is also here.
Wander down the docks here to dream about your next boat—no matter
what the size. Between the two piers, **Waterway No. 5** ends in grassy ter-
races that rise from water's edge.

Yale Landing at the south end of Lake Union

Puget Sound Maritime Historical Museum. Drop in here to savor salty remembrances of Seattle's past. Historical photos and models show Native American canoes, ships that once plied local waters, and lumber and fishing vessels built in area shipyards, as well as maritime artifacts. The museum also holds a library of books, charts, and posters, many of which are for sale.

A room in one of the buildings at Chandler's Cove temporarily houses the museum. The Puget Sound Maritime Historical Society, which preserves the region's maritime history, hopes to join Northwest Seaport at expanded facilities in a new Maritime Heritage Center in the nearby Naval Reserve Center building if the city of Seattle is successful in acquiring that property.

Waterway No. 4 and the Wooden Boat Center. Even if you don't know a catboat from a peapod, stop by here to get a real flavor of the lake. A covered pavilion at the end of Boren Avenue N and an adjacent dock in Waterway No. 4 house the Wooden Boat Center. There is no admission charge. The center itself is a combination museum, classroom, and small-boat rental site. Four traditional Native American canoes are suspended beneath the pavilion roof; other examples of wood craftsmanship, including rowboats and old water mains, are displayed on the adjoining lawn. Here the exhibits aren't locked in glass cases—you can actually examine them close up and even rent the boats for a spin around the lake.

Rental boats include a variety of classic pulling (rowing) boats that

The Wooden Boat Center has boats for rent.

traditionally were used for work, recreation, or racing; catboat and sloop day sailers include Beetlecats, Blanchard Jrs., and Lightnings. Sailboat rentals require a checkout to assure your sailing proficiency; however, you can rent a rowboat if you can pull on the oars. Then tour Lake Union in the same grand fashion that was popular with gentlemen in straw hats and ladies wielding parasols in the late 1800s. Rentals must stay on Lake Union. The center is open from 11:00 A.M. to 5:00 P.M. daily; closed Tuesdays. The rental portion is open slightly later in the day in summer.

The center offers numerous activities, many family oriented. Here you can learn to build a wooden boat, sail, navigate by the stars, or tie boaters' knots. The center houses a maritime library, and it periodically sponsors speaker's programs on marine history.

The Northwest Seaport Maritime Heritage Center. This nonprofit organization dedicated to the preservation and interpretation of the region's maritime history has offices as well as a gift shop, dory displays, and several workshops for volunteers in a building between the southeast end of South Lake Union Park and the Naval Reserve Center.

The group currently is working on the restoration of three ships: the schooner *Wawona,* the tug *Arthur Foss,* and the *Swiftsure* lightship. The three-masted schooner is moored at the lake's southwest corner, on the west side of Waterway No. 4. The *Arthur Foss,* which is seaworthy, sometimes is on display at other harbors around the area. The *Swiftsure*, which is currently moored in Ballard, is not yet open to tours because of its condition.

The *Wawona*, built in 1897, carried lumber and was also used for cod fishing. Born a sailing vessel, she remains one—the 169-foot schooner was never fitted for engine power throughout her long career. The 112-foot *Arthur Foss,* which was built in 1889, towed steamers and barges to Alaska during the Gold Rush and served as an active working tug on Washington waters and the Pacific Ocean. She even was a movie star, appearing in the 1933 movie *Tugboat Annie.* The tug was retired in 1968 and later was donated to Northwest Seaport. The 129-foot *Swiftsure,* one of the oldest lightships in the country, was built in 1904 and served as a lightship in the San Francisco Bay area

The Wawona *is undergoing major restoration at the Northwest Seaport Maritime Heritage Center.*

from 1929 to 1951. She then served as a relief lightship off the coast of Washington; she was decommissioned in 1960 and was declared a National Landmark in 1989.

Portions of the *Wawona* not under active restoration are open to the public. In addition to historic ship restoration, the Maritime Heritage Center offers marine history programs throughout the year, including marine chantey concerts and interpretive programs on maritime history and wooden ship construction techniques. Donations are welcome—and desperately needed to carry on the work.

South Lake Union Park and Waterway No. 3. For years the city of Seattle has considered several proposals for public parks at the south end of Lake Union. Some were grandiose, others more modest, but all coveted the property occupied by the Naval Reserve Center on the west side of Waterway No. 3. The city was able to acquire all the property at the lake's southwest corner except for the pocket held by the Navy. Under budgetary duress, the city took the least costly route in 1991 and developed South Lake Union Park, which wraps around the Navy property. The modest site's parking area, grass lot, picnic tables, and park benches are fine for sunning or snacking after taking in local sights.

Putting in a kayak for a paddle on Lake Union.

Waterway No. 3, on the park's north and east sides, is scheduled to eventually become a moorage for historic boats and will have a hand-carried boat launch. Until funds are available to develop it, the land sports moldering hunks of floats, occasional vagrant campsites, and a thick growth of blackberries.

Waterways No. 2 and No. 1
Access: Water

Waterway No. 2, an open, 160-foot-wide channel on the AGC Building's north side, runs along the shore south from the end of Lee Street. The bank is open and uncluttered; however, it drops steeply for 10 to 12 feet to a narrow rocky strip at water level, so there is no practical access from land.

Waterway No. 1, a broad, open waterway, has along its shore a pair of bramble-laden trestles of the now-defunct Burlington Northern Railroad spur line. Near shore, some broken floats and a few rotting pilings serve as perches for waterfowl. It is an interesting channel to visit by boat, but land approach is impossible.

Lake Union Undeveloped Street Ends

An abundance of streets terminate at the Lake Union shoreline; on many, although they are public, land approaches are not feasible because of high banks, dense growth, or other impediments. Such street ends on the lake's north side are at Latona Avenue N; on the east shore at East Edgar Street, East Louisa Street, and East Boston Street; on the south end at Terry Avenue N; and on the west shore at West Galer Street, Blaine Street, Crockett Street, Boston Street, Aurora Avenue N, and 5th Avenue N.

East Allison Street. This 100-foot-wide strip of shoreline at the end of East Allison Street is framed by a private marina dock on the south and a boat dealer on the north. The street's south half ends at a 4-foot-high stack of concrete blocks above a shallow, tapering beach, but the north half has a low timber bulkhead where paddlecraft can easily be dropped in. The channel might be difficult to spot from the water because the boat dealer frequently rafts yachts in the waterway. Parking is at the street end and along the north side of Allison's end, although spots here are frequently used by employees and customers of the dealer and marina.

Highland Street. A narrow channel on the AGC Building's south side on the east shore of Lake Union is unobtrusively marked as a "Public Shore." Three park benches line a narrow planting strip along the shoreline, and the bulkhead alongside the building can be used to tie up a few boats of patrons of the restaurant in the building's lower floor. Moorages on both sides of the street-end channel are private.

PORTAGE BAY AND THE MONTLAKE CUT

Portage Bay more than matches the eclectic mix of Lake Union. Along its edges are a wildlife marsh, yacht club moorages, a playground, houseboats, shore residences, and the University of Washington. A few marine-oriented businesses are concentrated along the northeast shore. Some public street ends wedged between private property provide an opportunity to reach the water to watch boating activity, launch hand-carried boats, or perhaps swim.

The bay is roughly 1/3 mile wide by 3/4 mile long, trending northwest–southeast. The major traffic channel runs along its north edge. Outside this dredged channel the bay ranges roughly from 8 to 20 feet deep, except for its south end, where it ends in a shallow brush and cattail marsh. This marsh offers paddle exploration amid birds and other water's edge critters. Raccoons and beavers might be spotted at dusk; waterfowl gather here in their fall migrations, and some nest here. The Highway 520 freeway crosses this marsh, elevated on piers. Boats will find good, well-protected anchorages in 10 feet of water, southeast of a line between the Seattle and Queen City Yacht Clubs, between the yacht club moorages and the Highway 520 viaduct.

At the east end of Portage Bay is the Montlake Cut, a 1/2-mile-long, concrete-walled canal. Portage Bay and Union Bay were originally separated by a low neck of land through which a stream intermittently flowed. This isthmus caused an annoying portage for early settlers navigating between Lake Washington and Lake Union. Coal transported from mines south of present-day Bellevue had to be transferred from barges to a tram, then back onto barges to negotiate the route. Sawmill-bound logs crossed the barrier via a small hand-dug flume. Although there were early efforts to dig a canal (some by hand with pick and shovel), the isthmus was not successfully cut through until 1916, when the channel was dug as part of the federally subsidized locks and Lake Washington Ship Canal project.

The Montlake Cut has red/green traffic lights at either end. When log booms that might fill most of the 100-foot-wide channel or other very large commercial boats approach, the lights will turn red; all other

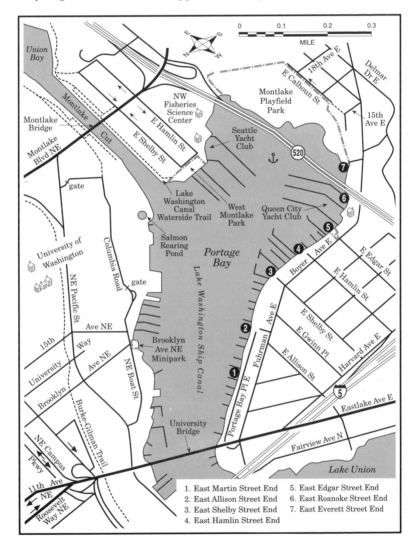

1. East Martin Street End
2. East Allison Street End
3. East Shelby Street End
4. East Hamlin Street End
5. East Edgar Street End
6. East Roanoke Street End
7. East Everett Street End

traffic, including small boats such as kayaks, must stand clear and not enter the channel until the green light shows.

On the first Saturday in May, Portage Bay hosts boats celebrating Opening Day of yachting season. Vessels of all types, polished and decorated to a fare-thee-well and sporting uniformed or costumed crews, gather here, awaiting the noon blast of the Seattle Yacht Club salute cannon and the ensuing procession through the Montlake Cut and past the anchored reviewing boat of the commodore of the yacht club. Thousands of onlookers line the shore to watch the colorful spectacle; an even larger crowd views the parade from boats tied to log booms in Union Bay. The cut is also the site of rowing regattas between UW crews and other universities.

The docks and roofed moorages of the Queen City Yacht Club, on the bay's southwest shore, and the Seattle Yacht Club on the southeast shore angle out, blanketing the water. These docks and adjoining parking lots are reserved for the use of members and guests. All summer long this portion of Portage Bay sees coveys of Optimists, Lasers, 420s, and Bights skittering to and fro as sailors, taking classes from the Seattle Yacht Club, learn to handle these one-person craft. The large brick building wedged between the Seattle Yacht Club and the freeway on-ramp is the Northwest Fisheries Science Center, a NOAA fisheries research laboratory.

Opening Day is great family fun.

Southwest Shore Street End Accesses (City of Seattle)

Access: Land, water

Several nice little street ends on Portage Bay exist because of the work of residents. Enjoy them, but show your appreciation by respecting private property and parking legally.

East Shelby Street. At the corner where Fuhrman Avenue E bends south and becomes Boyer Avenue E, intersecting East Shelby Street deadends at a small public access with a view into the Montlake Cut—in fact, the view from here and from farther up the street is often shown on local postcards. Stairs descending from the street end at a small lawn sandwiched between boat and houseboat docks. This is a favorite spot for watching Opening Day of the yachting season in May. In summer it is a nice place to swim and sunbathe (except for the problem of omnipresent goose droppings). Hand-carried boats can easily be launched here. Docks and property on either side of the street end are private; parking is very limited in the immediate area.

East Hamlin Street. One block farther south along Boyer Avenue E, a stub of intersecting East Hamlin Street ends at a barricade marked "Street End, No Swimming." Rock stepping-stones lead through shrubbery and past a pair of artfully placed concrete Japanese lanterns to a low bank at water's edge. A huge weeping willow leans out over a private little waterside hollow—a secret spot for reading, daydreaming, or perhaps an elfin tryst! A narrow path on the street end's south side ends at a gate to private property and more views across the bay to the Seattle Yacht Club. Parking is restricted to the north side of the short street-end block.

Cormorants on Portage Bay

East Edgar Street. In yet another block, just north of the Queen City Yacht Club, a concrete staircase leads down from Boyer Avenue E through carefully tended flowers and shrubs to another small grass-covered park. The park is dedicated to the memory of a neighbor girl who died in a skiing accident in 1981. A pair of benches invite a meditative stop, but most views are blocked by the adjacent houseboat and yacht club docks. The shallow water is a favorite spot for summertime wading and swimming.

East Roanoke Street. South of the Seattle Yacht Club the concrete deck of Highway 520 looms overhead. Here, the one-time street end has a twisted mat of blackberries covering a steep bank above the water. A footpath beaten through the encroaching vegetation to reach the water's edge permits local anglers to wander down to drop a line in the water. Property to the east, under the freeway, is signed "No Trespassing" by the Department of Transportation.

Montlake Playfield Park (City of Seattle)
Park Area: 28.1 acres
Access: Land, water
Facilities: Picnic tables, tennis courts, sports fields, recreation center, gymnasium, children's play equipment, rest rooms

A few acres of flat, grassy field atop reclaimed marshes form a playfield park at the southeast corner of Portage Bay. Most of the shoreline is separated from the sports fields by a brambly marsh. A clearing carved through the marsh at the park's northwest corner exposes a shallow, open beach for warm-weather wading. The park is on East Calhoun Street, between 16th Avenue E and 19th Avenue E. The park boundary extends west to include the wetlands near the freeway.

West Montlake Park (City of Seattle)
Park Area: 2 acres
Access: Land, water

A large lawn fronting the western edge of Portage Bay provides a choice spot for watching the annual Opening Day Yacht Parade and UW crew races through the Montlake Cut. A magnificent row of poplar trees lines the park's edge, interspersed with benches. The tapering beach is a favorite for summer wading and swimming. Use caution, as the beach is unguarded and heavy boat traffic can be hazardous.

Reach the park by turning east off Montlake Boulevard onto a one-way loop entering the area via East Hamlin Street and leaving via East Shelby Street. Parking is at a premium along the streets and might be restricted to residents during times of special activities. On Opening Day you'll have to park some distance away and walk or catch a bus to the site. The western end of the Lake Washington Canal Waterside Trail (described later) begins here, then heads east under the Montlake Bridge.

University of Washington: Lower Campus
The University of Washington occupies the north shore of Portage Bay, east from 15th Avenue NE. Its spacious campus was created as the hub of the 1909 Alaska-Yukon-Pacific Exposition (AYP), an entrepreneurial

A fish-rearing pond on the University of Washington campus

effort to put early-day Seattle on the world map. Prior to that time the university property was little more than uncleared forest, but the exposition left as its legacy the basic grounds of the university and several buildings.

Most of the waterfront along Portage Bay is devoted to oceanographic and fisheries activities. Docks and piers along the shore are interspersed with grass and trees; secluded pockets hold pleasant benches and picnic tables. Staircases descend from the Montlake Bridge's northwest corner and from adjoining campus facilities to the narrow walkway atop the cut's concrete bulkhead. Seats along the bulkhead are ideal for brown bagging while watching boat traffic, eye level with passing skippers. This area is crammed with onlookers during Opening Day or crew races.

West of the bridge, a canal-side beaten path leads to a large gravel pond near water's edge. This is a homing pond for university-maintained fall salmon runs and winter steelhead runs and a rearing pond for young salmon. Each May 120,000 chinook and 80,000 coho salmon are released from here in order to maintain runs for research and fisheries class projects. Seasonal spawning takes place here each Monday, Wednesday, and Friday from 10:30 A.M. to 12:30 P.M., from early October to mid-December. You can watch from benches that edge the pond.

West of Fisheries is the South Campus Center, where a waterfront picnic area is a choice spot to spend sunny days—doubtlessly discussing things of esoteric academic importance. Beyond here, a massive pier fronts the large Marine Sciences complex. Piles of exotic oceanographic equipment are often stacked on the dock, awaiting loading on the large research vessels that call this their home port. The university has long-range plans for converting the remainder of the waterfront along the north side of Portage Bay into a major expansion of the Fisheries and Oceanography facilities. These plans include a public car-top boat launch on Boat Street.

Sakuma Viewpoint (UW)
Access: Land

At Boat Street and Brooklyn Avenue NE a path leads downhill to a bulkhead fronting a 40-foot-square grass pocket, masked from the street by shrubs. Trees grow near the shore and benches line the path above the bulkhead; from one corner of the park a small wooden deck extends a few feet into the water. This is a quiet, secluded spot for a brown bag and a book, or perhaps some serious sunbathing. Nearby parking is usually crowded. A paddle club immediately to the east is the only place on Portage Bay where kayaks can be rented.

Portage Bay Street Ends
Street ends on Portage Bay that offer paddle access to the shore are at East Martin Street, East Allison Street, and East Everett Street. Due to difficult access, land approach is not feasible.

UNION BAY

Union Bay is the final link in the chain of waterways between the locks and Lake Washington. The 3/4-mile-wide bay is edged on both the north and south side by marshes. Boats of any draft must stay in the dredged channel, keeping a close eye on marker buoys. During football games large numbers of boats anchor on the bay's north side in 4 to 12 feet of water, then wave down shuttle boats to go ashore and cheer the Huskies. It's a grand, festive time of tailgate (or transom-gate) parties, and one that's uniquely Seattle. Anchoring is permitted only by participants, during events. Checking your depth sounder is recommended, or risk getting mired. If boating in the area, give a wide berth to large charter/tour boats.

But if you're among the yacht have-not's, the marshes offer endless delights of lily paddling and goose gandering by canoe or kayak. Anglers cast lines from boats and shore for crappie, perch, catfish, and both large and smallmouth bass that are abundant in the shallow water.

University of Washington Water Activities Center
Access: Land, water
Facilities: (General public) canoe and rowboat rentals, rest rooms; **(UW students, faculty, staff, and alumni only)** boat storage, sauna, locker rooms, lounge, yacht club, sailboats, sailing lessons, kayak club

Sunny days bring a steady stream of paddlers to the UW Water Activities Center where they can rent boats to poke into the maze of marshland channels along the sides of Union Bay. The center makes over 23,000 rentals annually—attesting to the popularity of paddling the local waters.

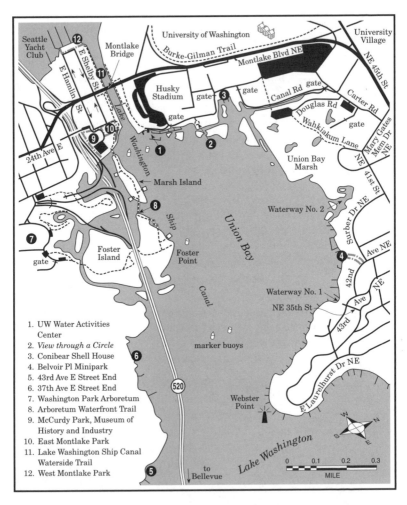

1. UW Water Activities Center
2. *View through a Circle*
3. Conibear Shell House
4. Belvoir Pl Minipark
5. 43rd Ave E Street End
6. 37th Ave E Street End
7. Washington Park Arboretum
8. Arboretum Waterfront Trail
9. McCurdy Park, Museum of History and Industry
10. East Montlake Park
11. Lake Washington Ship Canal Waterside Trail
12. West Montlake Park

Aluminum canoe or rowboat rentals are offered daily from 10:00 A.M. (9:00 A.M. on summer weekends) to dusk, February through October. All rental craft have paddles and approved life jackets. Boats may not be taken beyond the confines of Union Bay. The Water Activities Center is on Union Bay at the east end of the Montlake Cut, just below Husky Stadium. Parking (fee) is in nearby UW parking lots.

Union Bay Marsh (UW)

Just a wing tip away from the UW, a bird-filled marshland lies on the north side of Union Bay. For a good overview of the marsh, park near the UW Water Activities Center and walk north on gated Walla Walla Road, which runs between Husky practice fields and a narrow strip of junglelike

Stacks of canoes await renters at the University of Washington Water Activities Center.

shoreline. An unmarked path on the east side of the road leads to the *View through a Circle* earthwork. Here a 3-foot-diameter culvert provides a bore-sight view over Webster Point to the Cascades; climb the rough path to the top of the 20-foot-high mound for an overview of the tangle of narrow channels around tiny islands sprouting cattails.

After Walla Walla Road passes Conibear Shell House, take the next gated road to the east, Canal Road, which skirts intramural sports fields. At the next intersection, Wahkiakium Lane, a footbridge crosses the canal to parking lot E5. Marshland east of the canal is an ecological research area. Although much of the bog is a tangle of blackberries, brush, and cattails, a number of foot-beaten paths penetrate to wildlife viewing spots or narrow banks with water's edge views. Four ponds are edged by mounds of brush and grass that serve as nesting grounds for waterfowl. Walk quietly and be amazed at the number of bird species you see. Come time and again, as the inhabitants change with the season.

Trees and shrubs host hawks, owls, and a variety of sparrows. Reeds and cattails support red-winged blackbirds, swallows, marsh wrens, and warblers. Mergansers, scaups, buffleheads, grebes, gadwalls, and pintails fraternize in ponds with Canada geese and mallards. Some rest and winter here; others remain to nest and raise their broods. With patience a visitor might spot beavers, muskrats, turtles, or bullfrogs.

As an alternative to the land approach, rent a canoe at the Water Activities Center and paddle the narrow channels among the cattail islands. The narrow, bayoulike drainage canal (old Ravenna Creek) can be paddled, depending on deadfalls and debris, to the north end of parking lot E5 before it becomes impassable.

The Union Bay we see today is but a small vestige of the bay that existed here before 1916, when Lake Washington was lowered 9 feet with the opening of the Lake Washington Ship Canal. The edge of Union Bay prior to that time is roughly traced by the route of today's Burke-Gilman Trail, which follows the bed of now-abandoned rail lines that ran along the shores of the bay and Lake Washington.

With the lowering of the lake, the exposed fertile bottomland was used first for gardening, then as a site for the University Village Shopping Center. Marshland was drained for the ever-enlarging UW campus (including Husky Stadium); more bogs were devoured by a landfill garbage dump, which eventually was overlaid by UW parking lots and intramural sports fields. Finally, with increased environmental awareness, the value of wetlands became more appreciated. In 1991 the Union Bay Wildlife Habitat Management Area was created to protect and enhance the remaining wetland, bringing to an end its devastation.

Union Bay Marsh has a network of narrow channels.

Waterways No. 2 and No. 1 (UW, DNR)

Southwest of the intersection of Mary Gates Memorial Drive NE and Surber Drive NE, the slope drops away some 25 feet to a large brambled flat that once was a small cove at the outlet of Yesler Creek. Lowering the lake reduced **Waterway No. 2** to a tiny, shallow, lily pad–choked inlet surrounding a couple of cattail islands. Most of the former cove became a marsh which has over time become an impenetrable jungle of head-high blackberries interspersed with marshland shrubs. Check out the tiny inlet in a paddlecraft, but there is no possible access by land.

Waterway No. 1 can be accessed by land as well as water. To reach it, drive west on Mary Gates Memorial Drive NE toward Laurelhurst, and turn southwest on Surber Drive NE, then 42nd Avenue NE, and finally 43rd Avenue NE.

A great blue heron in Union Bay Marsh

On the west side of the road at the intersection of Northeast 35th and 43rd Avenue NE spot a basketball hoop at the head of a strip of undeveloped property, edged by a laurel hedge on one side and a fence on the other. A footpath leads across the grass to water's edge where riprap of broken concrete lines the shore. It would be possible to launch a paddlecraft into Union Bay from here.

Belvoir Place Minipark (City of Seattle)

Access: Land, water
Facilities: Dock

Between Waterway No. 2 and Waterway No. 1 is a city minipark amid the lawns of adjoining Laurelhurst homes. The 60-foot-wide park is a golf-course-smooth grassy strip between 42nd Avenue NE and a small indentation in the northeast corner of Union Bay. Tall firs shade the park's streetside end; at the no-bank shoreline a low, old 25-foot-long wooden dock extends outward. The signed park is on 42nd Ave NE, about 50 feet south of the intersection with Surber Drive NE.

Washington Park Arboretum (City of Seattle, UW)

Access: Land, water

Facilities: Paths, visitor center, greenhouse, Japanese teahouse, plant collections, benches, viewing and fishing platforms, rest rooms

The bulk of 200-acre Washington Park Arboretum stretches along a gentle hillside south of Union Bay. This beautifully landscaped green expanse holds the majority of the park's display of 5,500 different species of plants, as well as its visitor center, greenhouse, and Japanese teahouse. At its north end tip, the park tapers down to a maze of rush- and lily pad–choked channels, tiny islands, and two larger islands—Marsh and Foster.

While the arboretum's inland portion flourished after its founding in 1934, the marshy northern end remained fallow for many years. Debris fished out of lakes was dumped here for burning, and dirt and other landfill was piled onshore. In the 1960s, with an increased awareness of the value of wetlands, the marsh was recognized as the treasure it is. In 1967 a footpath was built through it, with footbridges joining Marsh and Foster Islands to the shore; however, because of heavy use over the years, portions of the spongy trail began to become one with the bog, and the path had to be closed. The route, which reopened in 1986, was rebuilt with firmer bedding and with sections on elevated boardwalks or floating concrete walkways. Even with the increased trail support, joggers and bicyclists are not permitted to use the trail because of the damage such heavy usage

Floating walkways thread through the marsh near Foster Island.

would cause. Pets are not permitted as this is a nature sanctuary.

By land or by water, exploration of this marshland is a delight. Canoes can be rented at the UW Waterfront Activities Center across the channel. Three broad, grassy, tree-lined peninsulas that thrust outward from the Arboretum's north end merge with the water in either low muddy banks or dense walls of blackberries, brush, reeds, and cattails. Narrow channels that wrap around these fingers of land connect pocket-sized bays that are often crowded with migratory waterfowl. Small islands—more collections of cattails than solid ground—harbor bird nesting areas, a heron rookery, and a beaver lodge. The shallow water holds crappie, perch, bass, chum, catfish, trout, and crawfish. Concrete piers sup-

The arboretum offers fine fishing for bass, perch, and catfish.

porting the deck of Highway 520 split the marsh from east to west, and highway off-ramps wend south to join city streets. Although these supporting piers might seem like civilized intrusions in a wild environment, they add to its labyrinth-like character.

Several parking areas are found along the marsh's north side; trails lead from them to the shore. A path from the end of East Foster Island Road crosses a footbridge over the narrow channel along the south side of the island, then continues northward down the heart of Foster Island, passes under the freeway, and ends at Foster Point at the island's northern tip. Aside from a partially open, 50-yard-wide swath on either side of the trail, the island is covered with a dense jungle of willows, birch, blackberries, and cattails. Foster Point offers views north across Union Bay to the UW campus, east to Lake Washington, with Cascades peaks rising above, and west to the twin summits of The Brothers in the Olympic Range, framed by the Montlake Cut. The ship canal's dredged channel is just offshore, and passing boats seem but an arm's length away.

A wooden observation deck off a spur path on the west shoulder of Foster Island provides a nice overview of the marsh area. On the marshy island's more solid portions a spongy path, bordered by planks and occasional benches, wends through willows, bulrushes, cattails, and water lilies. Twenty-seven numbered posts along the trail are keyed to a park map, available at either the Museum of History and Industry or the Arboretum Visitor Center, that describes birds and plants one might see at each spot.

Channels separating the mainland, Marsh Island, and Foster Island are spanned by floating concrete walkways, some with viewing/fishing platforms. Small bridges in the floating sections permit canoes and kayaks to pass into the marsh channels south of the freeway. Three spur paths on Marsh Island lead to concrete platforms for fishing, sightseeing, or lazing in the sun. The route ends at McCurdy Park, site of the Museum of History and Industry.

McCurdy Park (Museum of History and Industry and City of Seattle)
Park Area: 4.8 acres
Access: Land
Facilities: Museum, waterfront trail

At the Montlake Avenue end of the Arboretum Waterfront Trail one path goes straight ahead to a parking lot at McCurdy Park—more commonly known as the Museum of History and Industry (MOHAI). A second, ill-defined and muddy path continues to the northwest, skirting the edge of a pond set off from the ship canal by a thin islet; this path then merges with the Lake Washington Ship Canal Waterside Trail at the Montlake Cut's east side.

MOHAI, the dominant feature of the park, houses an impressive collection of historical documents and photographs, artifacts from pioneer days, and displays of Seattle's industrial development. Visitors can stroll past storefronts of an 1880s Seattle street, visit pioneer Henry Yesler's wharf, view model ships and period clothing, and hear the story of the Great Seattle Fire of 1889. A fee is charged to visit.

To reach the museum parking lot, two blocks south of the Montlake Bridge turn east onto East Lake Washington Boulevard. In 1½ blocks turn north on Park Drive (24th Avenue E) and follow it to the parking area on the museum's north side. A 5-inch, Mark 7 naval gun mounted at the edge of the parking lot is a lure for kids.

East Montlake Park (City of Seattle)
Park Area: 1.1 acres
Access: Land

Not as large or as heavily used as its counterpart, West Montlake Park, on the opposite side of the bridge, East Montlake Park is a strip of grass along East Park Drive between East Shelby and East Hamlin Streets. A bench and picnic table overlook McCurdy Park, MOHAI, and the section of the ship canal west of Foster Island. Still, it's a great spot to watch boating festivities such as Opening Day or the Christmas boats.

Lake Washington Ship Canal Waterside Trail
(U.S. Army Corps of Engineers)
Access: Land
Facilities: Footpaths, decks, benches, totem pole

A spur of the Arboretum Waterfront Trail leads northwest from the MOHAI parking lot to a broad wooden deck at the Montlake Cut's southeast entrance. Benches on the deck offer leisurely viewing of boat traffic through the canal. Above the deck is a tall totem pole, carved in 1937 by a Haida chief, John Wallace. The pole once stood at a cannery in Waterfall, Alaska; when the cannery closed it was brought to Seattle.

Paths lead from this deck up to East Montlake Park and west along the bank above the canal's south side. Halfway between the deck and the Montlake Bridge a concrete staircase drops to another small deck holding benches that overlook the cut's eastern entrance. From here the path along the canal's concrete bulkhead continues west beneath the bridge to West Montlake Park. Another long staircase just east of the bridge climbs steeply uphill, intersects the higher path, then continues climbing to street level at the bridge's southeast corner.

Union Bay Street Ends

The north street end of 43rd Avenue E is public; however, high bank and dense brush make beach access impossible.

37th Avenue E. Where East McGilvra Street meets the fence of the Broadmoor Golf Course at a T-intersection, an unmarked gravel road, 37th Avenue E, follows the fence line north to the shore of Union Bay. Here, amid shorefront blackberries, a narrow foot-beaten path offers access to the marshy shoreline. The view from the beach overlooks Highway 520 and the Nellie Cornish fountain which sits in the water near the freeway.

The Waterside Trail looks into the Montlake Cut.

CHAPTER TWO

LAKE WASHINGTON SOUTH

While Seattle calls Lake Union its own, Lake Washington belongs to many. In addition to sprawling Seattle, along its shores are two large cities, Renton and Bellevue, and numerous other smaller towns and communities. The glacier-gouged lake is 19½ miles long and generally 1¾ miles wide. Although it gently meanders north to south, its shoreline is fairly smooth, with only a few small bays indenting its more than 50 miles of shoreline. With only a few exceptions, the beaches are narrow, with the shore dropping off swiftly to the 30-foot level, then plunging to the lake bottom at 125 to 200 feet. At its south end, slender 5¼-mile-long Mercer Island rises steeply.

The main obstructions in the lake are man-made ones—bridges of floating concrete pontoons that cross it at two points. The Evergreen Point Bridge spans it midway, and the Mercer Island Bridge (actually a pair of parallel bridges) crosses the lake three-quarters of the way down its length. These bridges have elevated ends under which most boats can pass (see the introduction for bridge clearances). A small, 4-foot shoal with deadheads extends from Coleman Point on the lake's southeast shore, near Kennydale. Submerged rotted pilings exist at some points around the lake; anchor with care. The lake bottom tapers to 14 feet at its north end and becomes quite shoal off the mouth of the Sammamish River.

Lying beneath the lake waters are three sunken forests, believed to be the result of earthquake-caused landslides that occurred before the area was settled. Navigation charts indicate their location on the northeast lakeshore off St. Edward State Park (the Manitou forest), off the middle of Mercer Island's west shore, and off the island's southeast tip. Surprisingly, some of the trees are reported to be still standing and in relatively sound shape. Treetops that were a navigational hazard were removed when the lake was lowered; however, if you were to try to anchor at any of these places you would probably lose your hook—but these are unlikely spots to anchor, anyway.

Leschi Moorage on Lake Washington is overlooked by Mount Rainer.

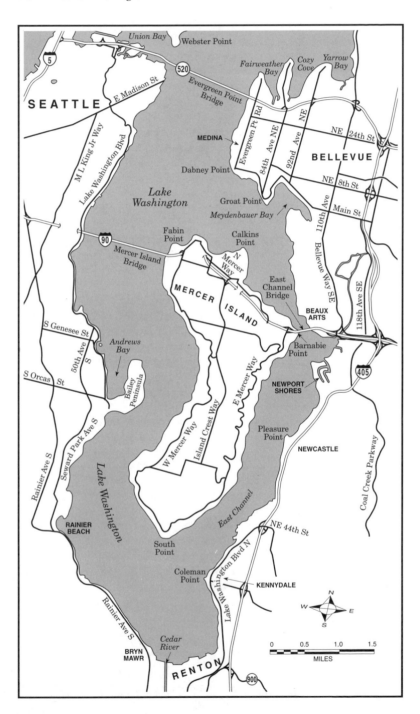

For sports anglers, the lake holds a wide variety of fish, including rainbow and cutthroat trout, steelhead, and kokanee. The mouths of the Sammamish River at the north end of the lake and the Cedar River at the south end offer excellent fishing for migrating salmon. Large and smallmouth bass, catfish, crappie, and perch are caught in the shallow water of Union Bay and the Mercer Slough.

THE WEST SHORE

The western side of Lake Washington south of the Evergreen Point Bridge has more public beaches than the rest of the lake combined. The city parks, fishing piers, and launch ramps on this stretch of shoreline are linked by Lake Washington Boulevard, a magnificent drive that follows the shore for 6 miles from Denny Blaine Park to Seward Park.

North Madison Park (City of Seattle)

Park Area: 4.5 acres
Access: Land
Facilities: Benches, swing set

This small park was originally part of larger Madison Park to the south, but was separated from it when Madison Street was cut through. Although it once held a municipal baseball field, its size has been significantly reduced. Large over-the-water multistoried apartment buildings enclose its sides, and a chain-link fence protecting the playground cuts off its beach access. It now offers only lake views, a set of swings, and a few park benches. To reach the park, from the intersection of East Madison Street and East 43rd Avenue, take 43rd (one-way north) for two blocks to its intersection with East Lynn Street, which meets the park at a T-intersection.

East Madison Street Dock (City of Seattle)

Access: Land, water
Facilities: Fishing pier, dock

On the north side of Madison Park, at the end of East Madison Street, an old dock that served as a ferry landing until the county ferry runs ended in the 1940s is now a fishing pier and boat dock. The tall, 65-foot-long pier provides views north over the nearby Evergreen Point Bridge to the Cascade Range, east to Medina, and south to Mount Rainier. A ladder on its end permits boaters to come ashore for supplies in the Madison Park shopping district a block away.

The short section of East Madison between East Howe and East 43rd Avenue is one-way southwest, requiring a digression via East Howe Street and East 43rd Avenue. The short 1/2-block street end above the dock has

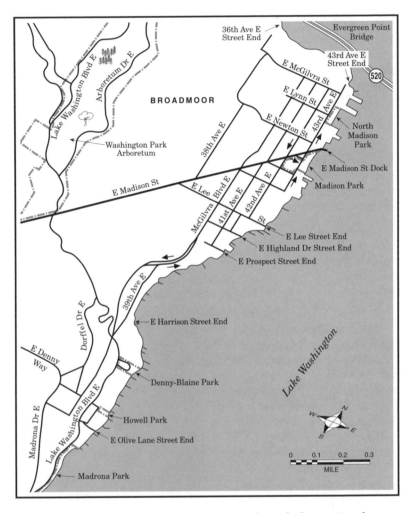

parking on either side, but space on the north might be restricted to use by tenants of adjacent apartments.

Madison Park (City of Seattle)

Park Area: 8.3 acres

Access: Land, water

Facilities: Swimming area (guarded in summer), swim floats with diving boards, bathhouse, rest rooms, tennis courts, benches, picnic table, children's play equipment

Busy Madison Park is bisected by 43rd Avenue E, dividing the park into two quite different sections. On the avenue's water side a broad, tiered lawn, framed with huge old trees, rolls gently down to a sandy swimming beach. On warm summer days throngs fill the lawn and roped-off swim area. When Seattle chills descend, beach visitors are mainly waterfowl or an occasional parent guarding a tot who can't resist playing in the sand. The bathhouse, which is open in summer, serves as a spot for community meetings off-season.

The park's larger, upland portion has play areas for adults (tennis courts) and kids (merry-go-round). The children's play area is worth a stop, whether you have toddlers in tow or not. Wooden beams on the climbing tower end with fanciful animal heads, and scattered groups of large, beautifully carved stone bears, cougars, and rabbits invite climbing—or just touching.

Fanciful animals inhabit Madison Park's playground.

Madison Park lies immediately south of the end of East Madison Street. Nearby streets are one-way to control traffic around this busy spot; watch for directional signs. Streetside parking is adequate, but not generous.

Denny-Blaine Park (City of Seattle)
Park Area: 2 acres
Access: Land, water

A sunbather's nirvana, this small greensward holds intimate sunning sites on three grassy tiers edged by rock bulkheads. Wall-like fences of neighboring homes enclose the sides, adding to the privacy. Below the lower bulkhead, the lawn tapers to a gravel beach. There is one drawback, however—there are no rest rooms. Panoramic views from the park's tiers spread west across the lake and over Bellevue high-rises to distant mountain peaks. To the south, snowy Mount Rainier floats above Mercer Island.

This is one of the early parks developed by enterprising realtors. While most of their contemporaries developed large-scale amusement parks on their plats, Charles Denny and Elbert Blaine favored a smaller "open-space" park. The original park's seawall enclosed a small oval lagoon with a boat launch ramp and wharf, and the lawn above displayed an elaborate fountain. The lake's lowering in 1916 left the lagoon and boating facilities high and dry. The old seawall is now the bulkhead above the park's lower tier.

Those Lake Washington Parks

Many things that are a nice part of the Seattle we enjoy today grew out of crass commercialism. This is especially true of the west shore of Lake Washington south of Union Bay, where eager land speculators used parks to draw dollars to this (then) remote side of the growing city. Recreation attractions were built at several points along the lake in the late 1880s. The most flamboyant of these were Madison Park and Leschi Park; others were at the sites of today's Denny-Blaine Park and Madrona Park.

John J. McGilvra, who homesteaded a large section of lakeshore, created the original Madison Park to lure prospective buyers to his lakeshore plats. The facility, which was reached via cable car, attracted thousands on summer weekends. It boasted beer and gambling establishments, a greenhouse, a promenade, baseball and football fields, a boathouse, piers, and a terminal for steamer rides on the lake. Bands and vaudeville acts performed on floating stages. Wooden platforms provided space where families could set up tents to enjoy week-long or all-summer stays.

An even larger park was at Leschi, 1¹/₂ miles to the south. To reach the park, a cable car running up Yesler Street from the city gave revelers a thrilling 3-mile-long almost roller-coaster trip over precarious trestles. The amusement park had a six-story casino with a theater featuring vaudeville acts. When the casino burned in 1893, it was replaced by an overwater pier with a dance pavilion. Later additions to Leschi Park included a floating bandstand, a boathouse with canoe and rowboat rentals, bathhouses to complement the fine swimming beach, ball fields, refreshment stands, a dock for sidewheel steamer tours of the lake, greenhouses, and a formal garden. A small zoo had sea lions and a panther; when it closed in 1903, the animals that were donated to the city formed

The stone bulkhead at Denny-Blaine Park marks the early level of Lake Washington.

the nucleus of today's Woodland Park Zoo. The parks' popularity was undeniable—40,000 people (about one-fifth of the entire city population) celebrated Independence Day at Leschi Park in 1908.

When the brash young city of Seattle decided to promote the AYP, the Olmsted Brothers, nationally acclaimed landscape architects, were hired in 1903 to plan a system of parks and parkways meandering from the exposition site (now the UW campus), through city property that later became the Washington Park Arboretum, and running south along Lake Washington, ultimately reaching Wetmore Cove (today's Genesee Park). At that time the city acquired several of today's lakeshore park sites as well as property through which the new boulevard would pass. Some property was from speculators who donated it, realizing the benefit of a fine boulevard fronting their platted land. The road, which was nearly completed by the time the exposition opened in 1909, provided easy land access to the lake.

By the early 1900s a fleet of small steamers that docked at the ends of the cable-car lines took people on scenic excursions as well as carting them to other recreation sites on the lake's east shore and on Mercer Island. Unfortunately, the completion of the locks and ship canal in 1916 lowered the Lake Washington water level by 9 feet, leaving the steamer docks high and dry. This, combined with the construction of roads around the ends of Lake Washington and the beginning of county-operated ferry service between Seattle's Madison Street and Kirkland and Medina, sounded the death knell for the excursion fleet. A single private ferry continued to run between Leschi and Mercer Island. Cable car rides, boat excursions, and grand amusement parks succumbed to the popularity of the automobile, and the old facilities were converted to much simpler city parks and bathing beaches. When the first floating bridge was completed in 1940, the Madison and Leschi ferries, last remnants of the once-proud excursion fleet, ended their service.

The lake's lowering added significant amounts of new waterfront to the parks; today the location of the old shoreline is evident in many locations as a tier in the lawn or an old bulkhead high above the present-day waterfront. As you enjoy today's parks, pause on this old lake rim to envision what it looked like more than 80 years ago, when mustachioed gentlemen and bonneted ladies with knickers-clad tykes strolled formal rose gardens, applauded brass bands on offshore floats, boarded steamers for lake excursions—and signed on the dotted line for wooded waterfront home sites. Perhaps your great-grandparents were among them.

The fountain is long gone, and that area is now the center of the parking lot loop. Visualize how this lovely little park must have looked in its 1910 heyday—still lovely, but in a much different way.

Reach the park by following Lake Washington Boulevard E either south from East Madison Street or north from Madrona Drive. At East Denny Blaine Place a road loop wraps around a slope above the parking area. The tiered park is below the parking lot bulkhead.

Madrona Park (City of Seattle)

Park Area: 16.3 acres
Access: Land, water
Facilities: Swimming beach (guarded in summer), swim floats with diving board, bathhouse, rest rooms, picnic tables, picnic shelter, benches, concession stand, play area, fishing pier

In summer, Madrona Park is like a median strip between two busy freeway lanes. On the land side walkers, joggers, and bicyclists (as well as cars) zip by along Lake Washington Boulevard E, while on the water side sailboats, cruising boats, and water-skiers skim along. Not that the park itself is a sea of calm—swimmers, sunbathers, picnickers, anglers, and kids all converge here on warm sunny days. This immensely popular family park fills a 10-block-long strip running south from East Pine Street all the way to Leschi Park.

Madrona Park boasts a fine beach for swimming and strolling.

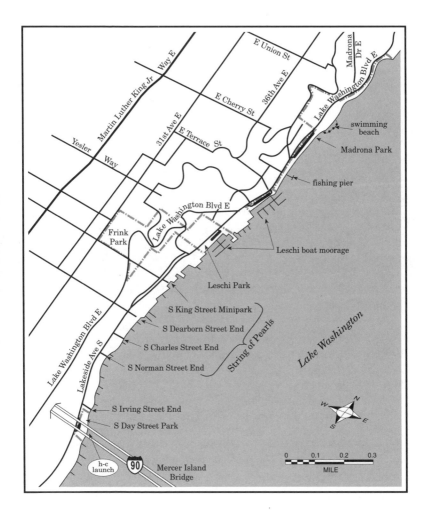

The city park's main portion lies south of the bus turnaround circle at Madrona Way. Here it drops from the street to lake level in two grassy layers, above a 4-foot-high bulkhead, where huge trees shade scattered picnic sites. Continuing south, the picnic area gives way to a swimming beach with two offshore swim platforms. Tangy smoke wafting from a concession stand's outdoor barbecue pit attracts a ravenous crowd. Devour your ribs on your sunny beach towel or in the nearby picnic shelter.

You wouldn't expect to find an ocean shore on Lake Washington, but there is one here. Between the bathhouse and a large parking lot lies a replica of a natural ocean beach. A neighborhood group, assisted by a city grant-in-aid, built this unique natural play area with sand, driftwood logs and a tile-lined stream bed that can be filled from the outpouring of

Leschi Park offers long-term moorage for boaters.

a nearby hand pump. Kids let their imaginations run free as they work the pump and create fantastic earthworks in the damp sand.

At the park's north end, stairs descend from the unmarked end of East Pine Street to a narrow grass strip above a high concrete bulkhead (no easy water access here). A beaten path runs south for three blocks; occasional breaks in the shoreline blackberry jungle permit anglers scramble access to a narrow, steeply sloped gravel beach. The main parking area is a large lot near the park's south end between East Jefferson and East Terrace Streets. A 120-foot-long T-shaped fishing pier juts into the lake near the parking lot's south end.

Leschi Park (City of Seattle)

Park Area: 15.2 acres
Access: Land, water
Facilities: Moorage (long-term only), dock, fishing pier, rest rooms, benches, tennis court

Today's offerings at Leschi Park are modest compared to its early days when an extravagant amusement park located here in the late 1800s included a casino, vaudeville theater, dance pavilion, elaborate gardens, and even a zoo. Today's city park facilities wrap around private waterfront businesses—offices, Corinthian Yacht Club, bicycle rentals, a deli, and shoreside restaurants (with more to come soon). Small boat moorages flank the commercial buildings and a swath of grass with park benches edges their south side. A large old dock, which now is a dandy fishing pier, is the remnant of the former landing for the ferry that operated here until the floating bridge was built.

Because of concern for landslides when the road was built, the route of Lake Washington Boulevard leaves the shore just north of Leschi Park and twists inland before returning to the water south of the Mercer Island Bridge. Lakeside Avenue S, which was built much later, runs along the shore for this 1¼-mile section. More than half the park lies on a broad lawn that sweeps up the undulating hillside between these two streets. Huge oak and hemlock trees frame flower beds, and paths wind uphill to a rest room, tennis court, and a few picnic tables. Its west edge joins Frink Park, which lies inland.

Leschi's String of Pearls

A few years ago, four public street ends along Lakeside Avenue were eyed by the Leschi Community Council for development as small shoreside viewing sites. Although some residents brought suit to prevent the improvements, the community council prevailed, and these pretty streetend miniparks, known as the "String of Pearls," were created. They are maintained by neighborhood groups; please show your appreciation by respecting the property and not blocking neighborhood parking.

South King Street Minipark. South King Street is the most northerly of the developed street ends along this side of Lake Washington. The stub end of South King Street, wedged between residences, ends at a small grass

A tiny park at South Charles Street is one of Leschi's String of Pearls.

enclave with a tiny brick-paved deck, landscaped shrubbery, posies, and a single bench. This is a pleasant spot for a picnic lunch while admiring boat traffic on the lake or taking a short break from bicycling the shore. Street-end parking is often crowded with neighbors' vehicles.

South Dearborn Street. At the east end of South Dearborn Street is a 60-foot-wide patch of lawn above a concrete bulkhead with no easy water access. A pair of park benches offer views of the lake and floating bridges. A few parking spots are available at the street end, but the large parking area to the north belongs to an apartment complex.

South Charles Street. A stub of South Charles Street ends at an attractive little grass plot; stepping stones lead to a park bench beneath the protective branches of miniature cherry trees. Views are west across the lake to the north end of Mercer Island. The beach below is gravel and cobble, and drops off rapidly, but it would be relatively easy to launch a paddlecraft here. Parking is scarce, as the street end is framed on both sides by private driveways.

South Norman Street. The perfect spot for an afternoon tête-à-tête, this tiny park has landscaping, a touch of grass, and a solitary park bench. Find it at the end of South Norman Street, framed by fences of adjoining residences. Street-end parking can accommodate only a couple of cars. The gently sloping beach could be used for launching paddlecraft or just for tossing pebbles in the water.

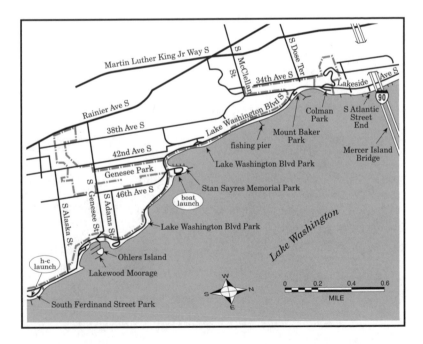

South Day Street Park (City of Seattle)

Park Area: 1 acre
Facilities: Fishing pier, hand-carried boat launch, sani-cans, *disabled access*

The park you see here today, directly under the north span of the Mercer Island Bridge, is a result of the building of the third (Homer M. Hadley) floating bridge. An old boat launch ramp had been at the site for many years. With the new bridge's completion, the redesigned park now sports a nifty water-level fishing deck and a paved path for putting in hand-carried boats. Both facilities offer disabled access from a parking lot just below Lakeside Avenue S. The stepped grass slope and plantings are a pleasant contrast to the concrete harshness of the freeway overhead.

Colman Park (City of Seattle)

Park Area: 27.3 acres
Facilities: Benches, view platform

After its brief inland trek, Lake Washington Boulevard returns to the shore in graceful curves that wind downhill through Colman Park. A broad lawn rolls down from the boulevard to a beach-side walkway that leads to a viewpoint edged by an ornate balustrade. To the north the tops of Bellevue office towers rise above the floating bridges. Across the lake the

Dad, daughter, and ducks enjoy Colman Park and its view of Mount Rainier.

Cascades form a backdrop for the wooded shore of Mercer Island, and to the south Mount Rainier looms high above Seward Park's Bailey Peninsula. Several huge old willows frame the shore, and benches line the top of low steps that drop to a cobble and gravel beach. The beach continues uninterrupted into neighboring Mount Baker Park.

The parking lot lies just below the intersection of Lake Washington Boulevard S and Lakeside Avenue S. A major portion of Colman Park lies inland; a path follows a wooded ravine uphill for several blocks to the park's nursery.

Mount Baker Park (City of Seattle)

Park Area: 18.5 acres
Facilities: Swimming beach (guarded in summer), pier, bathhouse, benches, picnic tables, tennis courts, Japanese garden, children's play equipment, rest rooms

Lake Washington Boulevard S splits Mount Baker Park into two sections, each with unique appeal. East of the street a sandy-shored cove wraps around the swimming beach, framed on the south and east by a long Y-shaped pier. This was the original hydroplane pit used for the Gold Cup races prior to the development of Stan Sayres Park to the south. Benches along the beach permit parents to supervise sand-digging toddlers. A few picnic tables dot the grass slope above the beach, which is divided into two levels by bulkheads. The lower bulkhead marks the shore prior to the 1916 lowering of the lake.

The pier at Mount Baker Park is a favorite for fishing or sunbathing.

The park's upland portion, on the west side of the street, surrounds a wooded gulch with a path that wends uphill to the south for four blocks, passing a historic Japanese garden. The concrete, multilevel Kobe lantern sits at the garden's lower end. Originally developed between 1912 and 1915, the garden surrounded a series of weirs that created small pools and miniature waterfalls in the creek draining the gully. The stream eroded the edges of the weirs, and after 40 years the pools and falls disappeared. Community groups, schools, and public agencies are now attempting to restore the garden. Continuing uphill, the ravine ends in an expanse of grass with tennis courts and an elaborate children's play area.

Mount Baker Park and adjacent Colman Park were the site of Seattle's first commercial water system. A steam-operated pump house, built in 1886 at the present site of the Mount Baker bathing beach, supplied fresh spring water from the hillside above to Seattle; later water was pumped from the lake and piped through hollow logs. Water was pumped from here to (vainly) douse the Great Seattle Fire of 1889. The old pump house now serves as the park's bathhouse.

Lake Washington Boulevard Park (City of Seattle)

Park Area: 204 acres
Access: Land, water
Facilities: Benches, picnic tables, fishing pier

Lake Washington Boulevard, one of Seattle's proudest legacies, was part of Seattle's efforts to gussy up the city for the 1909 AYP. The meandering parkway, with gracefully sweeping curves and waterfront vista, runs for a grand 9¼ miles all the way from Montlake Boulevard on the north to Seward Park on the south, linking numerous parks en route. The final

On Bicycle Weekends Lake Washington Boulevard is closed to vehicles.

leg, from Stan Sayres Park to Seward Park, was not built as part of the original boulevard, although the Olmstead Brothers, who designed the route, recommended its eventual construction.

The boulevard's most popular portion is a 5-mile section, designated as a city park, that connects Colman and Seward Parks. The tree-lined route follows the shore, first below wooded upland banks, then beneath a low inland bank lined with homes. A sidewalk edges the water side. Below it a grass slope drops to lake's edge, where at times a foot-beaten jogging path parallels the sidewalk. The beach area ranges from brushy high bank to tiny water-level peninsulas. An occasional bench or picnic table exploits wide spots in the lawn. Midway between Mount Baker and Stan Sayres Parks a T-shaped public fishing pier stretches into the lake. Endless views sweep across the lake to Mercer Island and the distant Cascades, and south to the Bailey Peninsula and the horizon-filling mass of Mount Rainier. This stretch of street is especially popular with throngs of bicyclists on designated "Bicycle Weekends"—the second Saturday and third Sunday of each month in spring and summer—when the boulevard and Seward Park are closed to vehicle traffic.

Stan Sayres Memorial Park (City of Seattle)

Park Area: 15 acres
Facilities: Boat launch ramps (fee), boarding floats, pier, floats and docks, rest rooms, rowing and sailing center

Fans of unlimited hydroplanes know Stan Sayres Park as the pit site for the "thunder boats" that race during Seattle's annual August Seafair celebration. Hydro driver and promoter Stan Sayres brought the Gold Cup

A hydroplane at Stan Sayres Memorial Park

races from Detroit to Seattle in 1950 and won the races here for five consecutive years. His exciting, newly designed *Slo-Mo-Shun* series of boats instilled "hydro fever" in Seattleites. When the original race site at Mount Baker Park became too congested, the Wetmore Cove site was dredged in 1957, creating the present hydro pits. The park is dedicated to Sayres, who died in 1955.

Races are held the first weekend in August. In less raucous periods, Sayres Park serves as one of three Parks Department boat launch ramps on this side of Lake Washington. Eight lanes of ramps, separated by a pair of boarding floats, drop off the peninsula's east side. Boat size limit is 25 feet; launching of PWCs is prohibited. A dock on the north tip can be used for brief stops. Parking for about 35 cars and trailers is at the center of the peninsula. The Mount Baker Rowing and Sailing Center, on the park's south shore, offers summer classes in shell rowing, small boat sailing, sailboarding, and canoeing and kayaking; rental sailboards and day sailers are available.

Lake Washington Boulevard originally ended here, at a small bay, until a trestle spanned the bay in 1912 and the road was extended to Seward Park. When the lake was lowered, it became a slough, and it was filled with dirt in the 1930s. (Sadly, there was no appreciation of wetlands in those days.)

Lakewood Moorage (City of Seattle)

Park Area: 14.6 acres
Access: Land, water
Facilities: Moorage (long-term only, fee)

A small cove sheltered by tiny Ohlers Island holds the three docks of the Lakewood Moorage. Use of the gated moorage and adjacent parking lot is restricted to rental patrons. The city acquired the property in 1910 in an agreement that specified that the 2,000 feet of waterfront would be used for a public boathouse. The current docks were built in 1952. On the cove's west side, a second parking lot off Lake Washington Boulevard S is public, as is the beach area below it. Here, low concrete stairs lead to a steep cobble beach.

South Ferdinand Street Park (City of Seattle)

Access: Land, water
Facilities: Hand-carried boat launch

This slight bulge into the west side of Andrews Bay, facing Seward Park, holds little more than a parking lot and a loading area. A 25-foot carry leads to a ramp and low-bank beach. Alongside the ramp, a low earth-fill pier makes climbing into kayaks and canoes easier. The remainder of the

park is a swampy shore where ducks and geese emerge from the marshland to try their hand (wing?) at freeloading from park visitors. The parking lot is accessible only from its south entrance. Water-skiing is prohibited
in Andrews Bay south of this point.

Seward Park (City of Seattle)

Park Area: 277.8 acres

Facilities: Swimming beach (guarded in summer), picnic tables, picnic
   shelters, rest rooms, fishing pier, trails, tennis courts, amphitheater,
   children's play equipment, Japanese garden, forest preserve, fish
   hatchery, art studio

It's hard to believe there still is virgin forest in Seattle, but here it is, in
one of the city's most splendid parks. As early as 1892 the nearly 1-mile-
long Bailey Peninsula was considered for a nature preserve. The Olmstead
Brothers recommended that the city acquire it, and in 1911 the city followed through by purchasing the property, assuring that much of it would
remain in its near-primeval state.

When the lake was lowered, bays became marshes, marshes became
land, and islands became peninsulas. The peninsula you see today was
once separated from the land by a soggy marsh that flooded when the

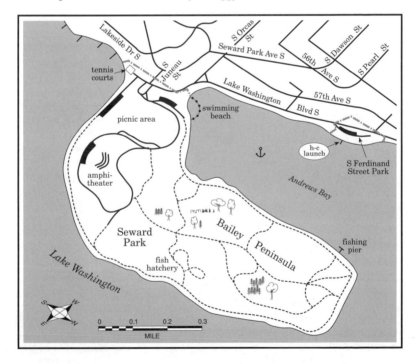

lake level was high. Because of its isolation, deer, beaver, muskrat, mink, and other wildlife remained here even after the mainland was becoming settled. Except for small mammals such as squirrels and shrews, all are gone today. Resident mink became *persona non grata* when they took to snacking at the fish-rearing ponds, so they were trapped and removed.

Because of its range of habitat, the park offers some of the most varied birdwatching in the metropolitan area. Several species of owls nest in the dense coniferous forest, and you might also spot woodland birds such as nuthatches, wrens, warblers, and vireos. Andrews Bay shelters waterfowl year-round, but it is especially interesting in fall and winter when migratory birds, including beautiful loons, drop by.

Nearly all the developments have been confined to the park's southern third, leaving the remainder wild. A 2¼-mile-long road once

A little waterfall flows from the outlet of the fish hatchery at Seward Park.

circled the peninsula's rim, but that has been closed to vehicles, and only walking, jogging, and bicycling are now permitted on it. A footpath that runs down the center of the peninsula has numerous branch paths leading to forest wonders—Douglas-firs 6 feet in diameter, ancient bigleaf maples, and jungles of sword ferns.

But that's not all the park has to offer. Most visitors don't leave the action at the park's south end, where there is a swimming beach and bathhouse at the head of Andrews Bay, picnic meadows with tables and shelters, and a children's play area. The Gateway of Welcome near the entrance is a reproduction of the torii gate at Miajama, Japan. It was donated by Yokohama citizens in appreciation of Seattle's aid following a 1923 earthquake. Pinoy Hill, in the heart of the park, was named by Seattle Filipinos who picnic there. A Greek-style amphitheater on the south side was used for orchestra and dance productions until traffic jams the concerts caused became unbearable for neighbors.

The peninsula's west side encloses Andrews Bay, a favorite anchorage for boaters—the only area on Lake Washington within the Seattle city

The road that circles Seward Park is fine for walking, jogging, or bicycling.

limits where anchoring is permitted. A pier once used by the Lake Washington steamer fleet is now a fishing pier reached by a short trail.

The park entrance is at the intersection of Lake Washington Boulevard and South Juneau Street. A short loop road through the picnic areas on the hill is the only road within the park remaining open.

Martha Washington Park (City of Seattle)

Park Area: 9.87 acres

This terrific piece of public property is a work in progress. As of 1998, plans are for the shore to be preserved as a natural area, with the remainder of the park supporting this role. Eventually, the meadowy upland, re-shaped by cuts and fills, will be restocked with native plants. Rebuilding of the wide strip above the low-bank beach will create two small coves, with the remainder of the beach protected by a riprap bulkhead. At the end of 57th Avenue S, which bounds the park's west and south sides, is a small drop-off/pick-up area with a gravel path leading to the beach; little else in the way of amenities is planned. The only parking is along South Warsaw Street, which runs along the property's north side.

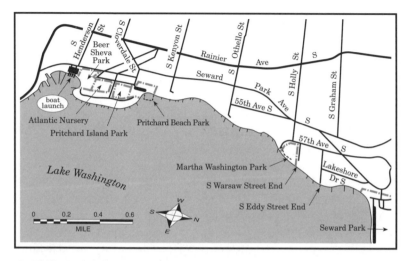

Pritchard Island Park (City of Seattle)

Park Area: 8.8 acres
Facilities: Swimming beach (guarded in summer), bathhouse

The three parts of Pritchard Island Park—Pritchard Beach Park, Pritchard Island Park, and the Atlantic Nursery—all occupy land that was once Dunlap Slough. Englishman Alfred J. Pritchard, who purchased the 2,000-foot-long island south of the Bailey Peninsula before the turn of the century, built a footbridge over the slough and created a forested estate on the shore. The mainland beach was so popular that by 1910 petitions were circulated to develop a bathing beach here. The lowering of Lake Washington significantly altered the area, causing the slough to dry and Pritchard Island to become one with the mainland. The island itself, unfortunately, never became a park; most of it is now private residences crammed along a single street. However, Atlantic City Park (Beer Sheva Park) crept slowly northward. By 1936 all the property extending to the north end of the former slough was city owned, and a park nursery was located there. The bathing beach was completed in 1940 as a Work Projects Administration project.

Pritchard Island Beach remains as popular as ever; recently renovated facilities include a parking lot and a modern bathhouse. Expanses of lawn taper down to a sandy beach and swimming area. The entrance to the beach area is from South Gratin Street, at 55th Avenue S. The former channel on the island's west side is now a grass-covered depression at the south end of the beach area. To the east, park property runs up to Island Drive S; here is only a street-end turnaround, with no parking permitted in the vicinity. The beautifully landscaped point of land at the former island's north tip provides a nice shaded spot to watch beach activities.

The portion of the old channel between the island and mainland that lies between the beach area and South Cloverdale Street is still called Pritchard Island Park. It is a broad swath of grass and landscaping, but it has no recreational amenities. The continuation of the old channel bottom south of South Cloverdale, which is still used as a park department nursery, has no public access.

Beer Sheva Park/Atlantic City Launch Ramp
(City of Seattle)

Park Area: 26.6 acres

Facilities: Boat launch ramps (fee) with boarding floats, rest rooms, children's play equipment

Beer Sheva Park, originally known as Atlantic City Park, was renamed in honor of Seattle's sister city in Israel. The excellent eight-lane launch ramp at the park's south edge, its most significant water-oriented feature, still bears the Atlantic City name. The cove was the site of the pioneer town of Rainier Beach and is said to be the birthplace of Princess Angeline, daughter of Chief Sealth for whom Seattle was named. Where the unlikely name of Atlantic City came from is a matter of speculation.

A short section of the park, with a fenced-off marshy shore on its north side, faces on the cove wrapping around the ramp area. Most of the park lies inland from the beach—a spacious grass field amid a scattering of old

The boat launch ramp at Beer Sheva Park

trees, a few park benches, a swing set, and a one-time (no longer) tennis court. Parking between the launch ramps and Seward Park Avenue S accommodates about 50 cars and trailers.

Street Ends on the Southwest Shore

Although a number of street ends along the lake's southwest shore are platted to the shore and legally public, none provide any usable public space, as all drop off steeply, beach is nonexistent, or shore debris makes them unusable. North of the Mercer Island bridge these street ends are at East Olive Lane and South Irving Street. By Colman Park the South Atlantic street end is public. Between Seward Park and Renton street ends are at South Eddy Street, South Warsaw Street, South Perry Street, South Norfolk Street, South Cooper Street, 72nd Avenue S, and 75th Avenue S.

East Lee Street. The east end of East Lee Street deadends at a barricade backed by a 12-foot-high laurel hedge. An obscure path at the hedge's north side leads to a 60-foot-wide, gently tapering, sand and cobble beach. This easy launch spot for paddlecraft would make a superb minipark if developed. From the water the street end can be identified by a "Cable Crossing" sign on the property. Park along Lee Street, but don't block private driveways.

East Highland Drive Street. This spot appears to be two driveways with a row of trees between them. Tall laurels hide the shore. Park carefully along the public (center) portion of the street end, and skirt the laurel hedge's south side, where a footpath picks its way through an 80-foot-wide mat of blackberries to a beautiful little shore area above a gently sloping gravel beach. As with the East Lee street end, this property can be identified from the water by a "Cable Crossing" sign.

East Prospect Street. From East Highland Drive, turn south onto 41st Avenue E, which meets a stub end of East Prospect Street at the fence along the north end of the Seattle Tennis Club. Park along a gravel road parallel to the fence. A narrow, paved lane drops down to an adjoining driveway and to water's edge. Easy water access makes the beach an ideal spot to launch paddlecraft, although parking is limited. Tangled blackberries have been cleared from the site and it has been seeded, although there are no other amenities. From the water, look for the street end just north of the tennis club. (Watch for tennis balls that have been lobbed over the fence bobbing in the water.)

East Harrison Street. From the five-way junction of 39th Avenue E, McGilvra Boulevard E, and Lake Washington Boulevard E, head north on 39th (signed "Local Access Only"). In a couple of blocks, look for a sign marking the cross-street of East Harrison. To the east, beyond what appears to be a landscaped private drive, a narrow path wends through dense trees and brush to a nice little street-end gravel beach with a sandy pocket on one side. There are no significant identifiers from the water.

East Howell Street. Although this is signed as a city park, it is only a broad shoreline street end at the foot of an overgrown bank that stretches 100 feet inland. At water's edge a small pocket of lawn above a gently sloping cobble beach sports a few trees that provide shade for an afternoon picnic. A narrow, sometimes muddy path leads down the steep bank from the short stub of East Howell Street below Lake Washington Boulevard E. From the water the park can be identified by a speed-limit marker buoy directly offshore.

MERCER ISLAND

Islands are traditionally seen as secluded retreats, and Mercer Island certainly started out that way. A luxurious resort with cottages and a 75-room turreted hotel was built on the island's northwest end in 1887 by C. C. Calkins to attract Seattle's well-to-do. Steamers brought the Gatsbys of the time to the resort to stay in its fine hotel and while away leisure hours in the formal garden with its greenhouses, fountains, and maze. The resort closed in 1902, victim of the 1893 depression, and the ornate hotel was destroyed by fire in 1908.

Once introduced to the island's beauty, Seattle's gentry began a slow influx, building country estates and vacation homes on the remote enclave. The first East Channel bridge, constructed in 1923 between Barnabie Point, on the island, and Enatai, on the lake's east shore, permitted residents to enjoy a 30- to 50-mile road "commute" to Seattle around either end of the lake, although steamers from Seattle continued to call at several island landings. With the construction of the first floating bridge in 1940, the island lost much of the isolation that had made it an attractive getaway. It became heavily settled, serving primarily as a bedroom community for Seattle and the Eastside.

The 5 1/4-mile-long island, which lies cupped in the south end of Lake Washington, rises steeply from water's edge to a forested, 350-foot-high backbone. Shores drop off sharply, and most beaches are narrow. Many parks and miniparks of today are at historic steamboat landings.

60th Avenue SE at the Mercer Island Bridge
(City of Mercer Island, Washington State DOT)
Access: Land, water

Between the two spans at the east end of the Mercer Island bridge lies the home port for a Department of Transportation (DOT) ship that patrols the bridge. The city of Mercer Island, in collaboration with the DOT, developed a pleasant little shoreline park just north of the DOT offices and dock.

A small parking lot adjacent to 60th Avenue SE fronts a lush grass

1. 60th Ave SE at I-90
2. Calkins Landing
3. Slater Park
4. Garfield Landing
5. Proctor Landing
6. Franklin Landing
7. SE 43rd Street End
8. Miller Landing
9. Groveland Beach Park
10. 85th Place SE
    Street End
11. Clarke Beach Park
12. City Boat Launch
13. Fruitland Landing
14. Luther Burbank Park
15. Lincoln Landing
16. 72nd Ave SE Street End
17. Roanoke Landing

carpet edged by a bed of wild roses. A path diagonals downhill, loops around a green knoll, then reaches a 4-foot-high boulder bulkhead that tapers to the water. It is possible to launch paddlecraft here, although the scramble over the rocky bulkhead is a bit difficult. The park is a nice spot to sprawl on the cool grass and spend a relaxing hour or two watching boats pass under the bridge and gulls soar overhead.

60th Avenue Southeast Miniparks

(City of Mercer Island)

Access: Land, water at all parks except Calkins Landing

Facilities: Swimming beaches (unguarded), benches, picnic table at Slater Park, dock at Proctor Landing, *disabled access at Slater Park*

Afternoon sun warms the beaches and shaded nooks of four little parks along a 1/4-mile stretch of Mercer Island's northwest shore. To reach the parks, leave I-90 at Exit 6 (eastbound only) or Exit 7 (Island Crest Way) westbound, and work your way west on any of several streets to West

Lake Washington's Floating (and Nonfloating) Bridges

You might not think that concrete can float, but that is the premise that allows Lake Washington's bridges to exist. All are built on a series of huge concrete pontoons, with air chambers designed to keep them afloat, that are linked together with cables and anchored to the lake bottom. Three of the world's five floating bridges are found here—the fourth is on Washington's Hood Canal, and the fifth is in Canada. The Evergreen Point Bridge is the longest in the world, at 7,578 feet, and the Homer M. Hadley span is the widest.

The soft mud bottom and the 200-foot depths of the lake between Seattle and Mercer Island for a time thwarted any plans to build bridges between the two shores. Engineer Homer Hadley first proposed a concrete pontoon bridge in 1921. The city and state then fought over the project for nearly 20 years, questioning whether it would actually work and calling it everything from "Hadley's Folly" to "a municipal eyesore," before the dream was realized. When it opened in June 1940, amid great hoopla and civic pride, the 1 1/2-mile-long structure was the longest floating object ever built, and the only floating bridge in the world.

The four-lane bridge, with sidewalks where people could cross on foot or bicycles, was wildly successful, carrying heavy loads of traffic between Seattle and the Eastside. Despite concerns that a pontoon bridge would be unstable, it proved solid and seaworthy, having to be closed only for brief periods when waves flung over the railing by severe storms made driving hazardous. The original bridge was designed with driving lanes diverted around an open center "bulge," into which one of the pontoons slid in order for

Mercer Way. Head south on West Mercer Way, then turn west on Southeast 28th Street. Calkins Landing is at the end of 28th, just beyond 60th Avenue SE. The other parks are south along 60th—Garfield Landing is at the end of SE 30th Street, and Proctor Landing is at the end of Southeast 32nd Street. Parking is in small parking lots or along the street.

Calkins Landing. In the early 1900s vacationers arrived via steamer at this small beach, then strolled to the nearby hotel operated by C. C. Calkins. The elaborate resort is only a memory, steamers no longer chug about the lake, and the former landing is now a tiny park with a swimming beach. A 200-foot-deep patch of well-tended grass at the street end, edged on the south by a grass path, reaches out to a 3-foot-high large boats to pass through. Unfortunately, this bulge became a driving hazard, causing a number of deaths of motorists who failed to negotiate the turn. It was removed in 1981, making the bridge solid. Only boats that can clear the elevated spans at the ends of the bridge, or that detour around to East Channel, can now reach the lake's south end.

The bridge caused an explosion of growth on the Eastside—so much growth, in fact, that in the 1960s a second floating bridge was built 5 miles to the north between Evergreen Point and Seattle's Montlake neighborhood. There were no questions this time as to whether it would float—only the concern that Lake Washington would ultimately be paved over. In 1989 a third span was added across the lake, this one parallel to the original Mercer Island Bridge. Appropriately, this bridge was named in honor of Homer M. Hadley, whose brilliant inspiration made all this possible.

Although the bridges have seen considerable drama and tragedy over the years, with deaths, births, and even ridiculous stunts occurring on them, the most terrifying event occurred in November of 1990 when the original bridge was undergoing major structural improvements. During a fierce storm with high wind and heavy rain, a number of pontoons took on water and sank, while other pontoons broke free and began to float away. The span had been shut down for the repair work, so no one was killed, although two workers had to run for their lives as what they described as a "gurgling monster" thrashed about and then settled to the bottom of the lake. The sinking was blamed on hatches left open during the repair work, which allowed water to enter the pontoons during the storm. The span was subsequently repaired with new pontoons; it now carries eastbound lanes of I-90.

log bulkhead. Below the bulkhead, the swim area begins at a shallow sand and gravel beach; roped-together floats mark deep water. A pair of benches permit parents to watch young swimmers. Because the roped off swimming area fills the shoreline, water access is not possible.

Slater Park. This beautiful little park has all that is needed for a perfect afternoon. A two-tiered lawn drops down to a low bank shore. Ivy, perennials, and shrubs border the walkway. At the lower level, birch, rhododendron, maple, and willow line the edges, and groups of comfortable benches are scattered about. Bring that novel you've been wanting to read, or pen and paper to begin the book you've been planning to write, and settle in.

Slater Park offers benches and sun-dappled lawn.

A log sunk in sand forms a low bulkhead above a sloping gravel beach. Paddlecraft can easily be launched here if wheels are available to make the 200-foot descent from the parking lot. No outstanding features identify the park from the water.

Garfield Landing. This is another former steamboat landing that now serves as a pleasant little minipark. A tree-edged creeklet gurgles along the south side of the street-end patch of lawn. The grass tapers down to a low bank, rock, and concrete bulkhead above a narrow gravel beach. This is an easy spot to launch a canoe or kayak for exploring up and down the Mercer Island shore. The only amenity here is a single wooden bench.

Proctor Landing. Yet another old steamer landing lives on as a street-end park. The chain-link fence and concrete wall that edge the property might seem unfriendly, but the park has one sought-after attraction—a dock. On the south side of the shallow, grassy beach is the 75-foot concrete dock, with 5 feet of water off the end.

The short carry from the parking lot makes it ideal for dropping in a kayak or other car-top boat, or for fishing. From the water it can be identified by the dock and a large "Cable Crossing" sign on shore. A path leads inland from here, following Southeast 32nd Street to parks at the island's center, and the business district.

West Side Public Accesses

Access: Land

A Metro sewer connection site might not sound like an appealing public access, but several exist along the Mercer Island shore; some are at former ferry landings. These street ends have no park improvements, but they are public property that affords shoreline access for viewing, fishing, and in some cases swimming (unguarded).

Franklin Landing. This small street-end site is a nice spot for a noon-time picnic, or splashing and wading, and has good scenery across the lake to the forest of Seward Park's Bailey Peninsula. A narrow grass strip drops to timber steps that breach the low bank. In early times island deer were known to swim across this 1-mile passage to snack on mainland grass, perhaps thinking the grass was greener on the other side of the water.

To reach the park, drive south on West Mercer Way to Boulevard Place, 0.1 mile south of the intersection of Southeast 40th Street. Continue on Boulevard Place for two blocks to Southeast 42nd Street; the landing is at the street end. There is no adjacent parking, making kayak launching difficult. The nearest streetside parking is about a block east on Boulevard Place.

Southeast 43rd Street. To reach this street end, turn off West Mercer Way onto Southeast 43rd Street. The street drops steeply from the north end of Forest Avenue SE for about a block to water level. Here a 40-foot-wide patch of concrete and weeds fronts the bouldered shoreline overlooking Seward Park. The lack of parking in the vicinity and the rocky shore make kayak launching impractical.

Miller Landing. Picture this spot when a little steamer would chug up to a dock to drop off mail or pick up island residents headed for mainland shopping. Although it is small and difficult to find, Miller Landing has a beach that can be used for picnicking, swimming (unguarded), fishing, or for watching boats in the channel between here and the Bailey Peninsula. Downtown Seattle buildings and distant Olympic Mountains line the horizon.

From the street end, a steep timber staircase and gravel path lined by trees drop to the narrow shoreline turf. To reach the landing from West Mercer Way, 0.8 mile south of the intersection of Southeast 40th Street, turn west on Merrimount Drive and then south on Forest Avenue SE. Follow Forest to its intersection with Southeast 81st Street; the steep narrow driveway downhill from this intersection leads to the park. The only parking is along Forest.

85th Place SE Street. At the island's extreme south end is another city street end with a sewer connection site. Parking at the street end can accommodate a couple of cars without blocking neighbors' driveways. Beach access is limited, and an approach from water is not appealing. At best, the access offers views south to the lake's end and the Renton waterfront, or perhaps a place to fish cold Lake Washington waters. The street end can be reached by turning south from East Mercer Way onto 85th Avenue SE and following the main road downhill to the water.

Groveland Beach Park (City of Mercer Island)

Park Area: 3 acres
Access: Land
Facilities: Swimming beach (guarded in summer), docks, rest rooms, bathhouse, picnic tables, children's play equipment

While secluded miniparks have their charms, for a family outing nothing beats a full-blown park with all the trappings. All summer long wading toddlers, sand-obsessed grade schoolers, bathing suit–clad teenagers, and sunbathing adults crowd Groveland Beach Park, the only fully developed park on the west side of Mercer Island. Although most of the Mercer Island shoreline drops off sharply, here a slight bay holds a sandy beach and water that warms enough for swimming.

In summer swimmers flock to Groveland Beach Park.

The popular swimming area, divided into shallow and deep portions, has a swim platform anchored in its center and a diving-board platform at the end of a dock. Docks and floats stretched between them enclose the swim area. Picnic tables scattered around the grass flat above the beach offer good views of the action. Year-round the docks offer fine fishing.

The steep, heavily wooded bank holds a large portion of the park. Here are more picnic sites and an elaborate children's play area. Parking is higher yet, on the bluff just inside the park entrance; wooded paths and a gated service road lead to the beach.

To reach the park, take West Mercer Way south from Exit 6 (eastbound only) off I-90, or Exit 7 (Island Crest Way) westbound, and work your way west on any of several streets to West Mercer Way. Turn west on Southeast 58th Street (one-way, westbound), which is signed to the park. The entrance and large parking lot are located just west of 80th Avenue NE.

Clarke Beach Park (City of Mercer Island)

Park Area: 9 acres
Access: Land, water
Facilities: Swimming beach (guarded in summer), wading areas, picnic tables, rest rooms, dock, fishing pier, sand play area

Mercer Islanders are proud of their fine parks, and Clarke Beach Park on the island's southeast side is certainly one of their finest. Paved footpaths weave downhill from the parking lot past rolling, shrub-lined lawns dotted with picnic tables.

A broad green slope near water's edge fronts two separate recreation areas. To the north, a concrete wall rimming a gravel-bottomed beach forms a children's wading area with a sand pit in a nook above. Farther south lies the main swimming area, with floats dividing it into shallow and deep portions. A concrete staircase leads from the bathhouse to the water. A 200-foot-long dock on the swimming area's south side has a diving board and ladders near its end, and a swim float is anchored in the deeper portion. Picnic tables on the grass above the swimming beach have close-up views of the action.

A dirt path leads south along the beach to a T-shaped fishing dock. A lone picnic site sits beneath trees at the head of the dock. The park, which faces on East Channel, has excellent views of Renton and the south end of Lake Washington. Looming above is the icy mound of Mount Rainier.

It would be possible to launch paddlecraft outside the designated swimming and wading beaches, but a set of wheels is recommended to move the craft from the parking lot to the beach area. To reach Clarke Beach Park, take Island Crest Way (Exit 7B eastbound, Exit 7 westbound) from I-90 and follow that road south for 3.3 miles to Southeast 68th Street and turn east. In a couple of blocks, bend right on Southeast 70th Place, and follow it to East Mercer Way. Turn south and reach the park entrance at Southeast 78th Street. A large parking lot is inside the entrance.

City Boat Launch (City of Mercer Island)

Access: Land, water
Facilities: Launch ramp (fee), dock, sani-can

When the I-90 freeway across Mercer Island was expanded in the late 1980s, money was included for improvements along the freeway right-of-way. One of these improvements was this public boat-launch ramp under the East Channel Bridge—the only one on Mercer Island. The loading dock adjoining the ramp also serves as the home port for the Mercer Island Marine Patrol boats. The two-lane ramp dips to the water on the bridge's south side; a large paved parking lot under the bridge accommodates about 75 cars and trailers. An on-site vending–machine dispenses parking tickets to be displayed on vehicles. Overflow parking is available in the City Hall parking lot, three blocks west on Southeast 36th Street, from 6:00 P.M. Friday to 10:00 P.M. Sunday. The ramp is open from 5:00 A.M. to 10:30 P.M.; no overnight parking is permitted.

To reach the launch ramp from either eastbound or westbound I-90, use Exit 8 (East Mercer Way) and take the first (well-marked) road to the east on the freeway's south side, which loops beneath the freeway to the ramp area.

Fruitland Landing (City of Mercer Island)

Access: Land, water

This former steamer landing takes you to another edge of the island, with different views. The minipark lies on the northeast side of Mercer Island on East Channel, due west of Beaux Arts. A 50-foot-wide strip of grass leads about 200 feet down to a low timber bulkhead that is a bit high, but it can be used for put-ins and take-outs of kayaks and other hand-carried boats. The shallow beach entices waders. A pair of benches above the shore look north into the entrance of Meydenbauer Bay and along the shore to the East Channel Bridge. The park is difficult to find, and unfortunately it has no parking; some limited parking can be found along the street in the block above.

To reach the landing, take Exit 8 (East Mercer Way) from I-90 and head west on Southeast 36th Street to North Mercer Way. Cross north over the freeway and immediately turn east on Southeast 35th Street, which in one block meets 96th Avenue SE at a T-intersection. Turn north on it, and in a short block, go east on Southeast 34th Street. In one block this meets 97th Avenue SE at a T-intersection. Turn north and in a short block reach the park at the street end.

Luther Burbank Park (King County)

Park Area: 77 acres

Access: Land, water

Facilities: Swimming beach (guarded in summer), picnic shelters, picnic tables (some reservable), barbecue stands, benches, rest rooms, trails, children's play equipment, tennis courts, volleyball area, game tables, docks, fishing pier, amphitheater, basketball hoop, county park headquarters, public art, wetlands, off-leash dog area

Luther Burbank Park has it all—picnicking and play areas for families, sports fields for the athletically inspired, swimming beach and lawns for sun worshipers, docks with moorage for boaters, piers for anglers, amphitheater for concert goers, and walking paths for nature lovers. This enormous diversity makes it the true jewel of Mercer Island parks.

The land was homesteaded by C. C. Calkins in 1887 (the same gentleman who built the resort on the island's northeast shore), and the Seattle School District purchased it in 1903 for an agricultural school. A concrete foundation near the park's north end marks the site of the school's dairy farm. The brick building that currently houses rest rooms by the dock area was the old boiler plant, and the brick parks-administration building was also once part of the school. The school, which was named for

The brick building by the moorage at Luther Burbank Park was once part of the agricultural school.

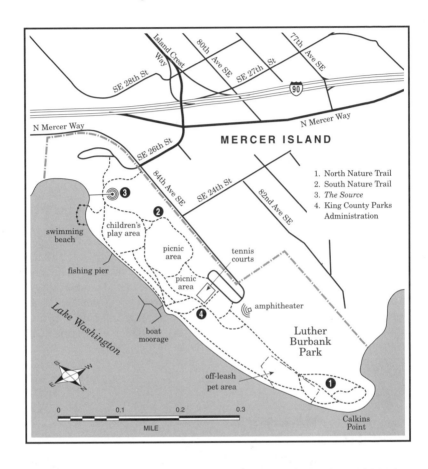

Luther Burbank Park looks north to the Evergreen Point Bridge and Seattle.

horticulturist Luther Burbank, closed in 1966. When the county acquired the property for a park, it retained the name.

With so much space, the park is able to scatter its facilities about, giving ample space to turn the kids loose or stage a family softball game without disrupting solitude seekers. Shaded picnic areas are in three different spots, play areas are at the park's center, and boat moorages, the fishing pier, and swimming areas are spread along the shore. A fenced-off northeast section of the park is presently part of a countywide experiment to provide off-leash exercise area for dogs. Its long-term use is under evaluation.

A large natural bowl near the north parking lot holds an amphitheater where concerts are staged at times; viewers sit on grass tiers that curve around a stage—also of grass. At the park's south end, a series of concentric grass-covered berms surround a native rock fountain whose water trickles down a channel to a marsh. This earth sculpture, *The Source,* is by artist John Hoge.

Unique posts at the Luther Burbank docks

Nature trails lace brushy and wooded areas of the park. The path around the north side passes through stands of native trees such as Alaska yellow cedar, red cedar, and Douglas-fir; English hawthorns and Lombardy poplar seen here are introduced species, planted by Calkins or the school. A chorus of chickadees, juncos, sparrows, and finches twitter in the understory. Marsh reeds and cattails host red-winged blackbirds and marsh wrens, and bald eagles and ospreys have been seen. Watch for evidence of beavers that cut down trees here and float them to the lodge they have built at the park's south end. Along the park's northeast side volunteers are restoring wetlands that once flourished here. Non-native species such as yellow iris and reed canary grass are being removed, and several small ponds are being increased in size to encourage reestablishment of native wetland species.

The South Nature Trail loops through fields and meadows. Apple trees planted here are reminders of when the park was an agricultural school. The varied habitat makes this a birdwatching heaven; walk slowly and you might see goldfinches, pine siskins, chickadees, flickers, or towhees.

Two entrances lead to the park. To reach the main parking lot near the heart of the park, take Exit 7 eastbound or Exit 7B westbound from I-90 (both marked as Island Crest Way). If eastbound, take Island Crest Way north across the freeway. On the freeway's north side, at the intersection of North Mercer Way and Southeast 26th Street, go east two blocks to the intersection with 84th Avenue SE. Here head north and arrive at the park entrance in about four blocks. To reach the south parking lot, turn south from the intersection of Southeast 26th and 84th SE, the entrance is on the road's east side in about a block. None of the lots are immediately adjacent to recreational facilities (except the tennis courts), so it is necessary to carry picnic or play gear a short distance.

North Side Public Accesses

Access: Land, water at Lincoln Landing
Facilities: Picnic tables at Lincoln Landing

Lincoln Landing. A long grass strip tapers north from the end of 76th Avenue SE to a low bank above the water. Four concrete steps lead to the beach. Amenities are just a pair of picnic tables in the grass above the shore; however, it is a nice spot for a picnic or wading, and it is ideal for launching paddlecraft for exploration of Meydenbauer Bay and the lake's east shore.

To reach Lincoln Landing, from the west take Exit 7A (77th Avenue SE) from I-90. Find 77th Avenue SE and cross northeast over the freeway, then head northwest on North Mercer Way. From the east take Exit 7 (Island Crest Way) to North Mercer Way and head northwest. In about three blocks, turn north on 76th Avenue SE, and follow it to the street-end minipark. Limited parking is available along the stub end of 76th.

72nd Avenue SE Street. A grass strip about 35 feet wide and 250 feet long stretches from the street end to a low bank above the water. No public amenities here, but the city mows and maintains the area with the active cooperation of neighbors. Would that all such public property were so graciously accepted!

Roanoke Landing. Once the major ferry stop on the Seattle–Mercer Island route, the busy landing is now but a memory. Roanoke Way is blocked 150 feet from the old ferry pier, and the remaining road ends atop a 10-foot-high bulkhead that once fronted the ferry pier and now provides views across the lake to the Leschi and Madrona areas. The steep bank offers no shore access. The landing can be reached by turning north from North Mercer Way onto Northwest Roanoke Way and following it a few blocks to the street-end barricade. Find limited parking along the street.

THE EAST SHORE

Cities and small communities spread along the southeastern side of Lake Washington, one rushing into the next with barely distinguishable boundaries. Tucked into corners along the shore between Renton and Bellevue are Newcastle, Beaux Arts, and Medina.

Cedar River Trail (City of Renton)

(Closed for river dredging and reconstruction during 1998)
Access: Land, water
Facilities: Boat launch ramp (nonmotorized boats only), benches, rest rooms, picnic shelter (reservable), picnic tables, basketball hoop, walking trail

This peaceful riverbank enclave provides a stark contrast to the sheet metal walls of the Boeing Renton Plant on the east and noisy planes at the Renton Municipal Airport on the west. The level, paved path winds along the Cedar River's east bank, ducking under road and freeway to reach Cedar River Park in 1³/4 miles. Earth mounds and shrubbery break the 100-foot-wide, tree-lined grass strip into people-sized nooks.

At the park's north end, about a hundred yards from the mouth of the Cedar River, is a single-lane concrete ramp for launching nonmotorized boats. Park adjacent to the ramp or around the perimeter of a park-end mound. Farther south along the trail are a picnic shelter, picnic tables,

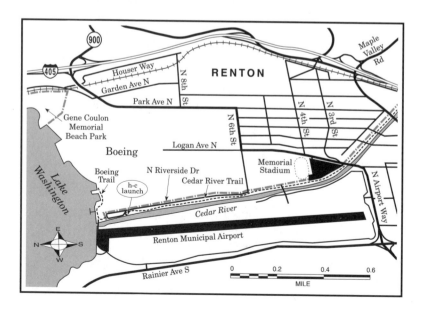

The Birth of Renton and the Eastside

The discovery of coal deposits near the mouth of the Duwamish River in 1853 and at Newcastle in 1863 triggered the Eastside's settlement and early growth. In those early days, getting the coal to market involved transporting it by wagon and canoe or loading it onto barges that were poled down the Black and Duwamish Rivers to Elliott Bay, a round trip of six days. When steamers began running on Lake Washington, coal cars were loaded on barges that were towed to Union Bay where they were transferred to a tram that crossed the Montlake isthmus. The coal cars were reloaded onto barges, carried to the end of Lake Union, then again offloaded to another tram that took them to Elliott Bay. From mine to waterfront the coal was handled 11 times!

Frustration over transporting coal led mine owners to build a narrow-gauge railroad line between Renton and Elliott Bay in 1877. The following year tracks were extended north to Newcastle and Coal Creek to reach the rich mines there. Labor disputes after World War I, coupled with a general switch to oil, caused many of the mines to close. Some continued on a small scale until 1963, and

basketball hoop, and rest rooms. Benches for watching the river roll by are scattered along the path.

To reach the picnic and launch ramp area, at the east side of Renton Memorial Stadium turn north from Airport Way onto Logan Avenue N. In four blocks turn west on North 6th Street, and follow it through the Boeing complex to a gate. Here it turns north and becomes North Riverside Drive as it runs along the park's east side. Alternatively, park in the large lot at the south side of Memorial Stadium, and walk the park trail north ¼ mile to the picnic and launch ramp.

Boeing Trail (City of Renton)

Access: Land, water
Facilities: Walkway, boathouse, rest rooms

A concrete walkway skimming above the shore just east of the mouth of the Cedar River gives anglers and walkers prime access to the south end of Lake Washington. Views run up the lake to the forested south end of Mercer Island. An old boathouse on the shore, once the home of Boeing-built hydrofoils, has been converted to rest rooms and a park boathouse where boat rentals and sailing lessons are offered.

one still carries on today—without the transportation problems the first mines faced. This early industrial growth undoubtedly set the tone for the area, as Renton remains heavily industrial today, with the commercial airplane division of Boeing filling the south shore along the Cedar River's east side (ironically, built on debris from Renton's coal-mining era).

As recently as the 1920s Bellevue was a remote farming community. Early development was thwarted by the difficulty in reaching it—early homesteaders had to thread their way up the shallow Duwamish and Black Rivers to Lake Washington, then follow crude roads north along the shore. Speculators homesteaded or bought land here, hoping for future railroad connections. Steamer access in the early 1900s attracted vacation property owners. By the late 1920s Bellevue had become a bedroom community for Seattle, with residents commuting from lakeside homes via ferries that crossed the lake. The completion of the first Lake Washington floating bridge in 1940 and the industrialization triggered by World War II ended the peaceful somnolence, and Bellevue and other Eastside communities experienced dramatic growth that still continues.

This, the first phase of a planned multiyear development of the park, was completed in 1997. Long-range plans call for extending the trail east around the end of the lake to Gene Coulon Memorial Beach Park. The entrance to the park is at the north end of North Riverside Drive; follow the driving directions for the Cedar River Trail.

Gene Coulon Memorial Beach Park (City of Renton)

Park Area: 57 acres
Access: Land, water
Facilities: Swimming beach (guarded in summer), bathhouse, picnic shelters (reservable), picnic tables, barbecues, picnic gallery, fast-food restaurants, volleyball courts, tennis courts, horseshoe pits, children's play equipment, rest rooms, boat launch ramps (fee) with boarding floats, guest moorage (fee), hand-carried boat launch, picnicking/fishing floats, fishing pier, sailboat and sailboard rentals, overwater walkways, walking path, botanical walk

Wow! A wealth of water, sun, nature, and play enhanced by well-laid-out facilities makes this the greatest park on Lake Washington. Coulon Park dramatically shows how modern planning can allow a site to very

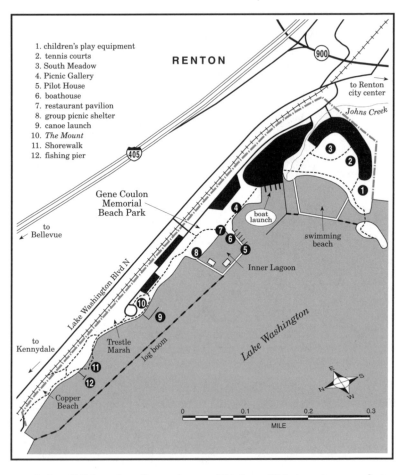

1. children's play equipment
2. tennis courts
3. South Meadow
4. Picnic Gallery
5. Pilot House
6. boathouse
7. restaurant pavilion
8. group picnic shelter
9. canoe launch
10. *The Mount*
11. Shorewalk
12. fishing pier

nearly be all things for all people—and it's beautiful, too. A covered picnic pavilion, overwater walkways, an elaborate picnic shelter, picnic floats, and a gracefully meandering path are only highlights of the handsome facilities.

The south entrance to the park is reached by exiting Highway 405 at Northeast Park Drive (Highway 900) and driving a short distance west to the intersection of Park Avenue N and Lake Washington Boulevard N. (From downtown Renton, head north on Park Avenue N to Lake Washington Boulevard.) Drive north on Lake Washington Boulevard for a short block to the entrance. The north entrance is a few blocks farther along the boulevard. Parking lots are jammed on weekends and holidays; informal roadside pull-offs along Lake Washington Boulevard serve as overflow parking.

The heavy action is at the park's south end where tennis and volleyball courts, horseshoe pits, and a large children's play area edge the beach. A concrete walking pier that rims the outside of the swimming area is open for fishing in fall and winter. West of the beach a boardwalk leads to a small shoreside island, designated as a bird sanctuary (although with the throngs of people, one wonders how many birds hang around here). Next to the swimming beach is the boat harbor, with an 8-lane boat launch ramp, boarding floats, 20 moorage slips, and a large parking lot. Fees are charged for parking, for launching and retrieving boats, tying up at the dock longer than four hours, or overnight stays in a mooring slip. The park is one of two spots on Lake Washington that offer overnight guest moorage; the other is Marina Park in Kirkland.

After the kids have worked up an appetite swimming or excavating sand, head for the park's center, where most of the picnic facilities are found. South of the enclosed Inner Lagoon is a block-long, two-level roofed picnic gallery with a view tower that offers a bird's-eye look at the park. Two pavilions on the shore north of the Picnic Gallery contain a pair of fast-food restaurants—burgers or fish 'n' chips, take your pick.

The concrete walkway surrounding the lagoon sprouts two floating platforms, ideal for fishing or private little picnics. Another roofed view

Floats on the Inner Lagoon at Gene Coulon Memorial Beach Park are fine for picnicking or snoozing.

Preparing to launch a sailboard at Gene Coulon Memorial Beach Park.

pavilion, the Pilot House, provides lofty views of boat activity from its vantage point at the lagoon's southwest corner. The lagoon itself is used for protected paddling; races are sometimes held here in a marked course. The high bank above the lagoon's north end walkway holds a 12-sided group picnic shelter with a central fire pit; outside decks offer additional picnic tables.

Continuing north, the activity begins to calm. The path weaves through groves of native trees and shrubs, with plant species identified. After passing the north park entrance (and parking lot), the trail winds around a high grassy mound and arrives at the canoe launch on Log Boom Pond. Put in paddlecraft here at the float, or rent sailboards or small sailboats at the Renton Sailing Club concession. The log boom that edges the pond minimizes waves and powerboat wakes; paddle in the calm comfort of the pond, or slip between logs for kayak excursions north to Kennydale and across to Mercer Island.

Drawing away from the vehicle-reached parts of the park, the path leads onward. A footbridge crosses a marsh where rail cars once dumped logs into the bay to be rafted. Farther on, the trail becomes Shorewalk, a boardwalk zigzagging over the water, then passes a long fishing pier poking into the lake. Proceeding north, the route crosses a marsh-bound creek, skirts a wide spot called Copper Beach (bench for resting), and then follows a wide grass shoreline to the north (walk-in) entrance.

Kennydale Beach Park (City of Renton)

Park Area: 1.76 acres
Access: Land
Facilities: Bathhouse, rest rooms, pier, swimming beach, picnic tables, children's play equipment

This small neighborhood swimming hole is sandwiched between railroad tracks and Lake Washington, and it is flanked by private residences. The swimming beach is a large, flat, treeless square of sandy fill above a concrete bulkhead, with a few picnic tables and some playground equipment. A concrete pier frames the south and west sides of the swimming area; a log boom outside the pier tempers wave and wake action (and prevents boat landings).

At the park's south corner, a small plot of grass that surrounds a bathhouse holds a few more picnic tables. The park, which is cut off from Lake Washington Boulevard N by railroad tracks, can be reached via a staircase crossing the tracks. Parking is along Burnett Avenue N or at a small lot uphill from the intersection of Lake Washington Boulevard and Burnett.

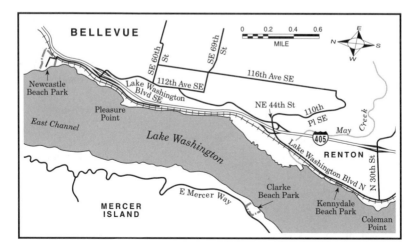

Young swimmers at Newcastle Beach Park

Newcastle Beach Park (City of Bellevue)

Park Area: 27 acres
Access: Land, water
Facilities: Swimming beach (guarded in summer), swim float, rest rooms, outside shower, pier with float, picnic tables, children's play equipment

Although the wide manicured lawn and sandy swimming beach are the features of Newcastle Park that you will first notice, nearly two-thirds of its acreage preserves one of the last natural habitats on the lake. The woodland harbors deer, and bald eagles might be spotted perched on the upper limbs of tall trees. Migratory waterfowl can be seen in season, and muskrats and river otters frequent undeveloped edges of the shore. A ³/₄-mile-long nature loop leaves from the turnaround area west of the parking lot, passing through cottonwoods, hawthorns, salmonberry, and alder. The property was logged in times past, but the wild is returning. Walk quietly and be rewarded by seeing birds and small creatures.

A flat, tree-lined asphalt path beside the grassy heart of the park leads from the parking lot to the beach. Near the beach, picnic tables are scattered about the open lawn and in the shade of trees, within view of kids turned loose in the nearby play area. A wide beach, defined by a low curved bulkhead, fronts the swimming area, and an L-shaped concrete pier protects the sides. Hand-carried boats and sailboards can be launched from a small float at the pier's end, or from the shore to the south, but launching is prohibited at the swimming beach. It is a two-block walk from the parking lot, so wheels are useful for moving boats to the beach.

Before the lake was lowered in 1916, most of today's park was underwater; a small cove indented the shoreline up to the present park entrance. Much of the bottomland exposed by the lowering was used for farming; a large dairy farm once was located just north of the park. In the surge of Eastside development in the 1960s (when Newport Shores came into being) the park's north half was platted for 14 single-family homes. Fortunately, the city of Bellevue acquired the property before the bulldozers moved in.

The park is reached by taking Exit 9 (112th SE) from Highway 405. At a T-intersection on the freeway's west side, turn north and follow this road for another ¼ mile to the park.

Southeast 40th Street Boat Launch (City of Bellevue)

Park Area: 2.5 acres
Access: Land, water
Facilities: Boat launch ramps (fee), boarding float, sani-cans, benches, *disabled access*

This pair of launching ramps for trailered boats is probably the most heavily used on the east side of Lake Washington, aside from those at Gene Coulon Park. From the north, approach via 118th Avenue SE, or from the south, take Exit 10 (Coal Creek, Factoria) from Highway 405

Bellevue's Southeast 40th Street Boat Launch is one of the most popular on the Eastside.

and head west. Coal Creek Parkway soon becomes Lake Washington Boulevard SE and then changes to 118th Avenue SE at the intersection with Southeast 40th Street. Southeast 40th is lined on the north by fences around boatyards and marine service companies. About 60 public parking spots on the road's south side are all reserved for vehicles with trailers. The only parking for vehicles without trailers are three spots near the head of the launch ramps; one is for disabled persons.

The two asphalt ramps are separated by a long boarding float. When the facility is busy, wait your turn in the westbound lane approaching the ramps. Tickets for use of the ramps can be purchased at a dispenser at the head of the ramps, or season passes are available from the Bellevue Parks Department. The only other amenities in the area are a pair of sani-cans and a few shoreside benches.

Mercer Slough Nature Park and Sweyolocken Boat Launch (City of Bellevue)

Park Area: 326 acres
Access: Land, water
Facilities: Hand-carried boat launch, bicycle trails, hiking trails, nature trails, visitor center, environmental education center, guided tours, sani-cans

Western pond turtles are part of the wildlife at Mercer Slough Nature Park.

Mercer Slough is an unexpected respite amid the freeways, office parks, and frenetic bustle of the city. Before the lowering of Lake Washington in 1916, the wetland was a large shallow bay. On its northern end a sawmill at Wilburton once operated, and several farms carved out of logging clearcuts rimmed the bay. Later, agriculture flourished around its edges. In the 1980s developers were poised to drain it and pave it over to make yet more office parks. In the nick of time residents formed the Save the Mercer Slough Committee and rescued it. Give mental thanks to these fine people as you wander the largest urban wetland in the state—which a real estate developer once called "unattractive, unfishable, and unproductive."

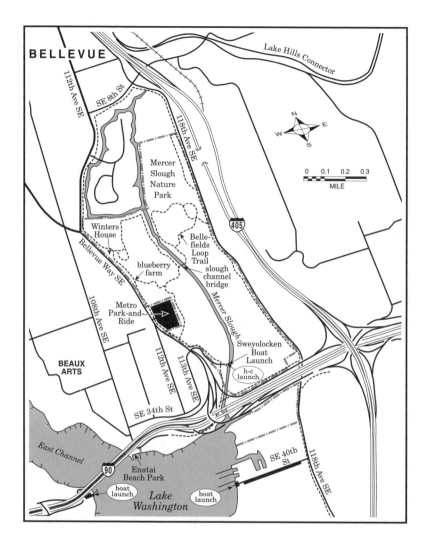

About a third of the slough today is leased as a blueberry farm, retaining its agricultural heritage. The remainder of the property is a nature park with boardwalk-spanned bogs and a narrow, reed-rimmed channel. The slow-moving creek is a favorite spot for canoeists and kayakers; motorboats are not permitted in the slough north of the boat launch. At the slough's southwest corner, Sweyolocken Boat Launch (hand-carried boats only) is on a tiny shallow cove with a low, dirt-filled boarding berm along one side. The marked entry road to the put-in area is on Bellevue Way SE at 113th Avenue SE. The road becomes on- and off-ramps for I-90 just a block to the south, so traffic can be a hazard at this turn. Kayaks and canoes can be rented at Enatai Beach Park, 0.25 mile west of the slough's mouth.

The channel, which arises from seepages of Richards and Kelsey Creeks, makes a nearly 1½-mile loop around the perimeter of civilized Bellefields Office Park, then enters the park and wanders south through the heart of the marsh for another mile. En route it ducks beneath a lacy metal footbridge that spans the slough, then passes under another footbridge and the concrete strands of I-90 before arriving at Lake Washington's East Channel. Tangled willow and Indian plum press against the 50-foot-wide channel. A sudden splash might herald an otter, turtle, or frog. The slower you go, the more you see: herons, fleets of waterfowl, red-winged blackbirds, marsh wrens, and hawks.

The park is equally fascinating to explore by land, with over 5 miles of trails and bikeways circling its edges and additional footpaths lacing the boggy interior. Several trail entry points are found at parking lots along the park's west side: one at the Sweyolocken Boat Launch (a good place for bicyclists to start), a second at the large bus park-and-ride lot, a third at the Overlake Blueberry farm, and a fourth at the Winters House Visitor Center. On the park's east side, trails start from a parking lot adjacent to 118th Avenue SE south of the Bellefields Office Park and at the park's southeast corner where there is parking along the street under I-90.

Much of the trail is built on elevated boardwalks that protect the delicate marsh and keep feet dry. On paths that are on the ground, notice how cushiony the surface is; this innerspring mattress of dead, compacted plants is a water-saturated peat bed, up to 80 feet thick, that has built up

Putting in a canoe at Sweyolocken Boat Launch

The slow-moving channel offers fine paddling at Mercer Slough Nature Park.

over the last 6,000 years. Plants now growing here will in time add to this rich earth, and new ones will spring from it. An interpretive nature trail at the slough's east side leads walkers past seven numbered sites displaying cattail marshes, woodpecker snags, decaying materials, and other features of the marsh. A booklet available at the trailhead at 118th Avenue SE and at the Winters House describes the habitats.

The historic Winters House at 2102 Bellevue Way SE houses the park Visitor Center. The California Mission–style home, built in 1929, was the first Bellevue building on the National Register of Historic Places; it can be viewed from 10:00 A.M. to 4:00 P.M. Monday through Saturday, and noon to 4:00 P.M. on Sunday. Brochures about the park and trails are available at the Visitor Center; free, guided nature-trail tours are conducted on weekends; and guided canoe trips (fee) are conducted from Sweyolocken. For details, call the Bellevue Parks and Recretion Department at the number listed in appendix A.

Enatai Beach Park (City of Bellevue)

Park Area: 3 acres
Access: Land, water
Facilities: Swimming beach (guarded in summer), dock, rest rooms, outside shower, picnic tables, canoe and kayak rentals

You might not think a city park could coexist with the elevated lanes of a massive freeway, but it manages to do so relatively well here. The park lies beneath I-90's East Channel Bridge, which links Mercer Island to Bellevue. The usual waterside fixtures of swim beach, sunning sites, and picnic tables are well represented here; as a bonus, a concession rents kayaks and canoes, offers paddling classes, and provides guided paddle trips in nearby Mercer Slough and along the east shore of Lake Washington. For rental and tour information, call the Bellevue Parks and Recreation Department at the number listed in appendix A.

The park's upper section is a perfectly manicured lawn above a 10-foot-high bulkhead. A deck on the roof of the kayak rental concession has picnic tables spotted along its edge; a concrete and wood framework over the deck echoes the nearby freeway spans.

Stairs drop down through the bulkhead to reach the shore, where low steps separate the wide sandy beach from the water. On the park's east side, a 200-foot-long pier that has swim ladders and raised sunbathing platforms at its end protects one side of the buoy-marked swimming area.

Kayaks and canoes can be rented at Enatai Beach Park.

On the west, a long concrete deck with several tables and lawn chairs fronts the concession rental's three-bay boathouse.

To reach Enatai Beach Park from Bellevue Way SE, take 108th Avenue SE south or 113th Avenue SE west. This latter street curves south, then bends west again to become Southeast 34th Street before meeting 108th at a T-intersection just north of the park entrance. Parking is under the freeway, at the entrance.

Chesterfield Beach Park (City of Bellevue)
Park Area: 0.6 acre
Access: Land, water
Facilities: Swimming beach (guarded in summer)

This tiny swimming beach on the east side of Lake Washington is a secluded treasure. From the parking area, a grass slope drops down a 120-foot-high bank. Occasional flat spots hold a shaded picnic table or two. A switchbacking staircase relieves the steepness of the descent to the beach, where a shake-roofed pavilion is edged by a living-room-sized grass plot. An 80-foot-long, L-shaped dock extending from the narrow park's north side has swim ladders along its inner side. The steep hillside down to the beach makes it impossible to carry boats to be put in, but paddlers exploring the shore can pause here for a leg-stretching lunch.

To reach the park, take 108th Avenue SE south from Bellevue Way SE, then turn west on Southeast 25th Street. In 0.5 mile, 25th bends sharply north becoming 100th Avenue SE. The park, obscurely signed, is located at this corner. Diagonal parking slots for five cars are available at the head of the park.

Burrows Landing Park (City of Bellevue)
Park Area: 0.25 acre
Access: Land, water
Facilities: Dock

This early-day steamer stop on the east shore of Lake Washington is now just a tiny park at the barricaded end of Southeast 15th Street. A short flagstone path leads to an 80-foot-long wooden dock with a swim ladder. The boulder bulkhead along the beach slopes steeply into a gravel beach that drops off rapidly. Although this might be used as a hand-carried boat launch site, the high steep bulkhead and limited street parking makes it less than ideal.

Reach the park by turning west off Bellevue Way SE onto Southeast 16th Street and following it to a T-intersection at 100th Avenue SE. Turn north here, and in one block head west on Southeast 15th Street, which deadends at the landing.

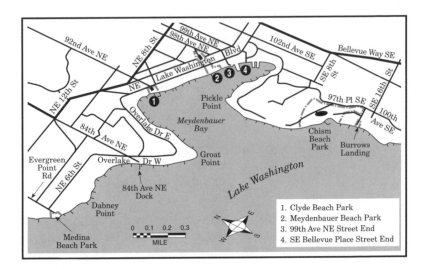

Chism Beach Park (City of Bellevue)

Park Area: 18 acres

Access: Land, water

Facilities: Swimming beach (guarded in summer), dock, swim float, picnic tables, children's play equipment, rest rooms, *disabled access*

Swim, kayak, picnic, swing, dig in the sand, toss a Frisbee, fish, or just laze in the sun—Chism Beach Park is the place for simple summer fun. A large grassy bowl serves as a natural amphitheater for watching swimming beach action or absorbing the sweeping vista of the Seattle skyline rising above coveys of sailboats on Lake Washington. Below the bowl, a semicircular concrete bulkhead wraps a cove that holds the sandy beach and swimming area. A 100-foot-long dock, with an L-shaped extension to the south, rims the swim beach's north side, and a swim float is anchored near the center of the cove. Picnic tables, a children's play area, and a lifeguard station line the shore. Fishing is usually excellent off the end of the dock.

A long staircase and serpentine ramp lead from uphill parking lots. The ramp is intended for disabled use; however, it is steep and rutted and might be an eventful ride. Fortunately, there is also a disabled-accessible entrance to the park from the south, with a pair of parking spaces just above the beach. The upper ramp does permit wheeling paddlecraft down to the beach, where launching is permitted (except for June through Labor Day, when the beach is reserved for swimming).

Road access to the park is rather complex, and at the time the area was surveyed for this book, it was complicated by landslides that closed 97th Place SE above the park. To reach the main (north) entrance to the park, turn west off Bellevue Way SE onto Southeast 8th Street. Follow 8th to 100th Avenue SE, then jog north on 100th Avenue SE, west on Southeast 7th Street, and then south on 99th Avenue SE, which progressively becomes 98th, and then 97th, before reaching Shoreland Drive SE, signed to the park. Turn downhill on Shoreland to the park entrance at Southeast 11th Street. To reach the disabled entrance, turn west from Bellevue Way SE onto Southeast 16th Street and follow it to 100th Avenue SE. Here turn north, and in one block head west on Southeast 15th Street. Turn north again on 96th Avenue SE to reach the park entrance.

Meydenbauer Bay

Meydenbauer Bay is a 1½ mile-long, foot-shaped pocket on the east side of Lake Washington north of Mercer Island. Surrounding hillsides rise sharply for 100 to 200 feet above the water and drop off almost as sharply to 70 to 80 feet of water depth; only at its southeast "toe" end does the bay gradually taper, offering a shallower shelf with 10 to 40 feet of water.

After the locks and ship canal were opened in 1917, whaling ships passed the off-season in Meydenbauer Bay in order to let nature do some boat maintenance by killing with freshwater the accumulated saltwater barnacles and teredo worms that attacked the hulls. Despite great anticipation after the opening of the ship canal, the expansion of shipbuilding and marine-oriented businesses at Meydenbauer Bay failed to occur, and it remained a quiet residential community. Today layers of homes are stacked along the surrounding slopes, while the bay's shallow southeast end holds marinas and a yacht club.

Although development has altered the bay with concrete bulkheads, rows of docks, and some areas of nearly wall-to-wall boathouses, a visit by water still evokes awe at the seclusion the bay must have provided before the Eastside exploded with growth.

Meydenbauer Beach Park (City of Bellevue)

Park Area: 2.8 acres
Access: Land, water
Facilities: Swimming beach (guarded in summer), dock, picnic tables, children's play equipment, rest rooms, outside shower, *disabled access*

A drive down a 100-foot-deep, steep ravine on the northeast side of Meydenbauer Bay leads to cozy Meydenbauer Beach Park. Huge old red cedar and Douglas-fir, some over 150 feet tall, shade a greensward that runs down the gulch and ends at a strip of lawn with picnic tables and pretty benches above the shore. The sandy beach faces the swimming area, edged by a long L-shaped dock and an offshore swim float. Low concrete steps that drop into the water invite future Olympic hopefuls to try

Future Olympians test the water at Meydenbauer Beach Park.

their first tentative dog paddling. Tucked away in a flat above the beach, a children's play area has a neighboring staircase leading to a small flagpole-centered deck that overlooks the beach, much like a ship's quarter-deck.

On the grass strip at the bottom of the ravine are poles for volleyball nets and a pair of disabled-accessible parking spaces with an easy paved path to the beach. Paddlecraft are not permitted to be launched during the swimming season of June through Labor Day; however, at other times they can be put in here. The long but gentle walkway from the main parking area to the beach makes it feasible to wheel them to water's edge.

The land approach to the park is rather obscure. Northeast Lake Washington Boulevard, which you might expect to be the access road, crosses a viaduct high above the ravine. To reach the park, turn northeast from Lake Washington Boulevard onto 99th Avenue NE. In a block turn northwest on Northeast 1st Street, which bends north as 98th Avenue NE in another short block. One more block to the north, at the park gate, 98th

Place NE heads southwest, dropping sharply to the main parking lot midway down the ravine. A side road continues downhill to two disabled parking spaces a short distance from the shore. A steep staircase also descends from the southeast end of the Lake Washington Boulevard viaduct to the disabled parking area.

Clyde Beach Park (City of Bellevue)

Park Area: 4.25 acres
Access: Land, water
Facilities: Swimming beach (guarded in summer), docks, rest rooms, children's play equipment, picnic tables, hand-carried boat launch, summer sailing program, *disabled access*

This charming little Bellevue city park hosts summertime crowds of swimmers, picnickers, and would-be Captain Hooks. A broad grassy bowl that drops from Lake Washington Boulevard to a 200-foot-wide beach area stops briefly at a mid-slope children's play area where a fanciful pirate ship, complete with (plastic) South Sea palm trees, holds forth. The shore is divided into two sections. To the south a concrete walkway arcs around a wide swath of grass with several picnic tables. Edging the beach is a concrete bulkhead with a decorative railing that evokes ocean waves.

Clyde Beach Park has a fine beach and unique play equipment.

The park's north section has the usual L-shaped dock protecting the swimming area. Low concrete steps lead into the water at the sand-bottomed swimming area. Nonmotorized craft may be launched south of the dock, but they are not permitted in the swim area.

As of 1998, more park improvements are scheduled. A cottage on the property's south side will be remodeled as a lifeguard station, and a large wooden pier and boathouse on the south and west side of the beach is slated to be reconstructed for park-offered day-sailing classes. The large vessel often moored at the dock, the *Argo*, belongs to the Sea Scouts.

To reach the park by land, take Northeast 8th Street west from Highway 405 through downtown Bellevue. Turn south on 92nd Avenue NE, which in two blocks intersects Northeast Lake Washington Boulevard at the park entrance. The park's northeast corner holds a parking lot for a dozen cars; a few additional parking spots, some disabled reserved, are near the beach.

Meydenbauer Bay Street Ends

A pair of street ends on the west shore of Meydenbauer Bay offer water views, but nothing in the way of improvements.

Southeast Bellevue Place. At the south end of metropolitan Bellevue, at the intersection of 100th Avenue NE and Main Street, Southeast Bellevue Place heads south, twisting downhill to a dead end at some condos. A narrow strip of grass here drops to a boulder bulkhead and a shorefront channel between private docks. Parking for a couple of cars is available at the street end. This is primarily a site to view the narrow south end of Meydenbauer Bay and its acres of boathouses.

99th Avenue NE Street. This street end is signed on Northeast Lake Washington Boulevard as a public waterfront viewpoint. A small swatch of grass at the west end of 99th Avenue NE sits above a steep 20-foot-high bank. Tangled blackberries make water access impossible. The street end lies between the docks of the Meydenbauer Bay Yacht Club and a private marina (which the city of Bellevue would like to acquire and turn into a public park—only money stands in the way). Until the Greenback Gods appear, the site is only a picnic site, with limited parking along the street above.

84th Avenue NE Dock (City of Medina)

Access: Land, water
Facilities: Dock

The lakeshore between Groat Point and the Evergreen Point Bridge lies within the boundaries of the city of Medina. As early as the 1890s fine estates lined this shore, fostering the nickname of the "Gold Coast." This reputation has been enhanced in recent years by the construction of the waterfront compound of billionaire Microsoft founder Bill Gates and mansions of other multimillionaires.

An obscure, little-known Medina public dock pokes out from the eastern shoreline of Lake Washington between Groat and Dabney Points. The 75-foot-long dock and its narrow, 30-foot-wide beach frontage are not easy to find from either land or water, and the only amenity is a dock with a swim ladder (day-use only). Good views here are of mountains, city skylines, and water. It is possible, but difficult, to carry a paddlecraft down the narrow path and stairs to the beach for launching.

To find the dock from the water, look for a private dock with a boat shed over the end. The public dock is immediately north. A harbor-line marker buoy lies about 100 yards directly off the dock's end. On shore, a tree-covered strip is sandwiched between adjoining residential lawns.

By land, follow the directions to Medina Beach Park; at the intersection of Northeast 12th Street and 84th Avenue NE, continue south on 84th. A block south of its intersection with Overlake Drive W, 84th ends. Streetside parking is available here for a few cars. A narrow footpath wends downhill between a fence and the brambled hillside to stairs leading to the dock.

Medina Beach Park (City of Medina)

Access: Land, water
Facilities: Swimming beach (guarded in summer), swim float, picnic tables, barbecues, benches, dock, hand-carried boat launch, rest rooms

In spite of the wealth displayed by Medina waterfront homes, the city hall at Dabney Point occupies a modest 1920s ferry terminal above a pretty little public park and swimming beach. The remnants of the old ferry dock provide some limited space for short-term boat moorage. Paddlecraft can be launched and retrieved here. At the park's north side, the tree-shaded lawn merges with a wide sandy beach, framed on the south by a man-made peninsula of boulders extending toward a swim float. The remainder of the swim area is outlined by a rope of floats.

Picnickers and sunbathers enjoy vistas across the lake to the west with the spikes of downtown Seattle skyscrapers along the horizon. To the south, Mount Rainier's icy mass forms a backdrop for the north end of Mercer Island.

To reach the park, take the 84th Avenue NE exit from Highway 520 and continue south on 84th to Northeast 12th Street. Turn west on 12th, and in about eight blocks head south on Evergreen Point Road, reaching the park in another six blocks. The intersection of 12th and 84th can also be reached by taking Northeast 8th Street west through downtown Bellevue from Highway 405. Parking in the vicinity is limited, and several spaces are reserved during weekdays for city hall business.

CHAPTER THREE

LAKE WASHINGTON NORTH

THE WEST SHORE

The north shore of Lake Washington between Webster Point and the mouth of the Sammamish River is mostly covered by small communities such as Sheridan Beach, Laurelhurst, and Windermere, with residences ranging from modest to massive. Aside from a few undeveloped street ends, the major public beaches along this portion of the lake are at Magnuson and Matthews Beach Parks and Tracey Owen Station. Popular Burke-Gilman Trail follows an abandoned railroad grade from the UW campus to Tracey Owen Station at the lake's north end, then continues up the Sammamish River.

Burke-Gilman Trail: UW to Kenmore (City of Seattle)

Access: Land
Facilities: Multi-use trail, benches, *disabled access*

Tracks for the Seattle, Lake Shore and Eastern Railroad (SL&E) were originally laid along the edge of Lake Washington, but when the lake was lowered in 1916, the beachfront moved outward. Thus, depending upon the place, the Burke-Gilman Trail, which follows the railroad grade, is now between 200 feet and 1/4 mile from the lake. The SL&E eventually merged with the Burlington Northern, which ran trains along the line for many years. Traffic dwindled, and Burlington Northern finally abandoned this section in 1971; the railbed was acquired by the City of Seattle and King County for the trail. This 11 3/4-mile section of the trail runs from the north edge of the UW campus to Tracy Owen Station in Kenmore. From there it continues into Redmond for another mile, where it joins the Sammamish River Trail at Blyth Park. Accesses are from any of the many streets the route crosses.

The Burke-Gilman Trail's southern section was described in chapter 1. After leaving the UW's lower campus, the path swings around the west

A boardwalk wanders through the marshland at Juanita Bay Park.

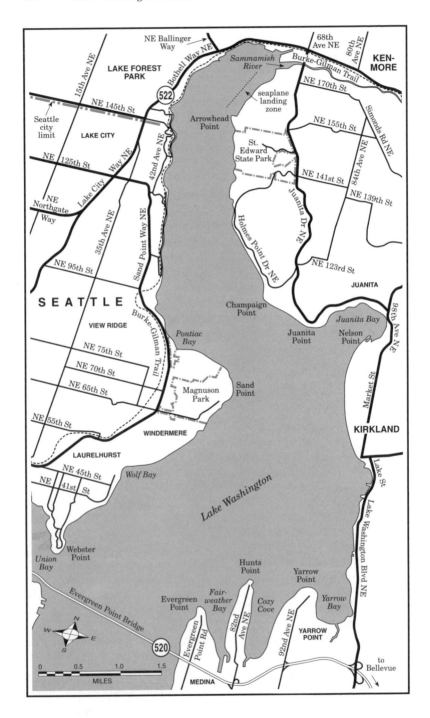

Fine sailing on the northern reaches of Lake Washington

and north sides of the University Village Shopping Center, which was an underwater part of Union Bay at the time the railroad track was laid. From here the railroad ran inland of the Laurelhurst and Sand Point peninsulas and rejoined the shore on the north side of Sand Point near Pontiac Bay. As the trail heads north, sometimes near the shore, sometimes a few blocks from it, lake views vary from tree-framed glimpses of blue water and white boats to panoramas of mountains, shore, and lake rendered in misty tones.

At Northeast 52nd Street the route edges the west side of an inland playground, Burke-Gilman Park, (Aaah . . . rest rooms and drinking fountains!) The path nears Magnuson Park 3½ miles from the UW campus. To reach the park, follow Northeast 65th Street east for a block. Continuing north, the Burke-Gilman Trail bends around Matthews Beach, and 1¼ miles from Magnuson Park it crosses a trestle over Sand Point Way. A short side path heads into Matthews Beach Park (more rest rooms and drinking fountains). Following the former lakeshore closely now, the path runs by tightly packed waterfront residences that lie below and ever-steepening wooded banks that rise to the west; only a few cross streets provide accesses. In 7 more miles Tracy Owen Station and lake's end are reached.

West Shore Street Ends

A few public street ends touch the northwest shore of Lake Washington. One at 51st Avenue NE is primarily used as a parking area for the adjoining private community beach club and has no beach access. At a few others it is possible to reach the water.

Northeast 31st Street. At the intersection of East Laurelhurst Drive NE and Northeast 31st Street, a sidewalk between two residences leads to a 70-foot-wide strip of grass above a low-bank beach. Part of the street end has been incorporated into the driveway of an adjoining residence. The spot offers a nice view, but has no improvements.

Northeast 43rd Street. At the intersection of Northeast 43rd Street and 55th Avenue NE, three flights of concrete stairs between dense hedges lead down the steep hillside, reaching a dirt path. A magnificent old cedar and a large willow shade the small beachfront area, where a 2-foot-high bulkhead meets the water. Offshore are rows of rotted pilings. It would be feasible to come ashore from a paddlecraft to stretch legs for a few minutes. The long staircase makes launching here unattractive.

Northeast 130th Street. This 60-foot-wide, low-bank lot between two residences at the end of Northeast 130th Street can be reached from the Burke-Gilman Trail. A short beaten path leads from the trail, crosses Riviera Place NE, and drops to water's edge. Riviera Place deadends to the north, and Riviera Place south of Northeast 132nd Street is a private road, so there is no feasible public access to the street end by car.

Northeast 135th Street. Another narrow break in shoreside residences has three parking spots along Riviera Place NE, all usually occupied by adjoining residents. A low-bank beach below a narrow strip of land offers water access.

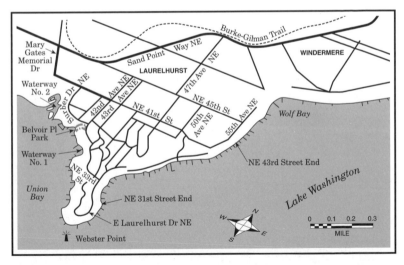

Magnuson Park (City of Seattle)

Park Area: 93.7 acres

Facilities: (Magnuson Park) Beaches, swimming beach (guarded in summer), swim platform, wading pool, sports fields, kite hill, paths, tennis courts, picnic shelters (reservable), barbecues, picnic tables (some reservable), boat launch ramps (fee), boarding floats, concessions (limited), rest rooms, view tower, off-leash dog area, *disabled access*; **(North Shore Recreation Area)** Art and cultural center, hand-carried boat launch, docks, float, concession boat storage, paths, picnic shelter, *disabled access*

Fort Casey State Park and Fort Worden State Park, along with Seattle's Discovery Park and numerous other fine parks in the Pacific Northwest, are the legacies of former Army installations. Magnuson Park, on 1½ miles of prime shoreline on the west side of Lake Washington, has a similar heritage, although in this case the park is the descendant of a Navy air station. Had the government not locked the land up during Seattle's early years, this probably would now be an exclusive residential enclave.

The airstrip the county created at Sand Point in 1920 was taken over by the Navy four years later. In the spring of that year history was made when four open-cockpit Douglas World Cruisers set off from here in an attempt to make the first around-the-world flight. Five months and 26,345 miles later, three returned successfully—the fourth had crashed in Alaska.

Sailboarding off Magnuson Park.

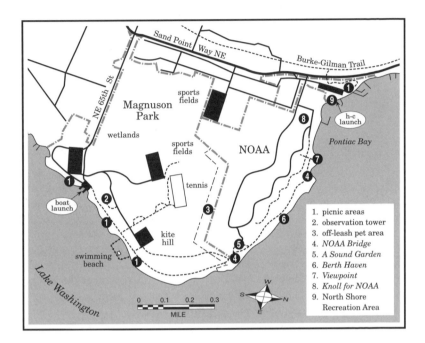

Over time the Navy appropriated the entire peninsula, and it was actively used during World War II and the Korean conflict. However, the peninsula's boggy underpinnings caused continuous settling of the runway, which had to be resurfaced periodically; in places the asphalt became several feet thick.

In 1970 the air station was deactivated and portions of it were surplused. A donnybrook ensued between the community (which wanted a park), the county (which wanted an airstrip), and NOAA (which wanted a site for regional headquarters). Because NOAA had legal priority as a federal agency, it claimed a large chunk of the surplused land. Wily U.S. Senator Warren G. Magnuson tacked an amendment on the surplusing bill pro-hibiting use of the property as an airport; a 1974 Seattle vote also rejected the airport proposal. The portion of the property not claimed by NOAA became a city park in 1977, and it (fittingly) was named after the senator.

Over the last 20 years the park has been a work-in-progress, and it will continue to be for a while. The remaining Navy property and buildings, which were surplused in 1997, will soon see a variety of social, ecological, and recreational uses: housing for homeless people will be built, the UW plans to use existing buildings for student family housing, an arts and cultural center will be focused on an old airplane hanger, and sports fields and natural wetlands will fill portions of the open land. A former Navy tank farm on Pontiac Bay, northwest of the NOAA facility, is scheduled to

The Many Lives of Carkeek Park

Sand Point was a primeval forested peninsula in 1875 when build-ing contractor Morgan J. Carkeek and his wife bought the north-ern 23 acres facing on Pontiac Bay. Tiny Mud Lake, lying southeast of their property, was filled with panfish, and herons searched its shallows for frogs. The surrounding forest was home to deer, otter, beaver, and muskrat. The Carkeeks built their estate here and en-joyed the beautiful site for over 40 years. Even though it was well north of the city limits at the time, in 1918 they deeded the land to Seattle for a campground where Seattleites could "rough it."

Fate began to show its hand in 1920 when the county cleared land south of the park for a small airstrip. In spite of planes buzz-ing about, and the continued enlargement of the airstrip over the years, Carkeek Park hung on, providing outdoor adventures for increasingly cosmopolitan youngsters. In 1926 the Navy took over all of Sand Point and purchased the park property. The park's log cabins were barged across the lake to King County's O. O. Denny Park north of Kirkland, where they carried on Carkeek's tradition in the youth camp that operated there. Sadly, the pristine forest and pretty little lake succumbed to bulldozers and concrete.

But, you say, there *is* a Carkeek Park in Seattle. Right! Money received from the sale of the Pontiac Bay property to the Navy was used to purchase property for today's Carkeek Park in northwest Seattle. And history has come full circle—the original Carkeek Park on Pontiac Bay has been reborn as a portion of Magnuson Park.

become the North Shore Recreation Area, an 11½-acre boating-oriented outpost of Magnuson Park. Old docks will be converted for use by small recreational boats, a hand-carried boat launch is planned, and small boat storage and sailing classes will be available.

The entrance to the main section of Magnuson Park is at the intersec-tion of NE 65th Street and Sand Point Way NE. At this south end of the park is a two-lane boat launch ramp with boarding floats and a large park-ing lot for cars and trailers. From here a walking and bicycling path fol-lows the shore north to the park boundary, then loops back to join the entry road's gated end. Picnic shelters, tables, and barbecues are scattered above the beach.

An old control tower on the shore now serves as an observation plat-form, giving 360-degree views of the spacious park, the end of Lake Wash-ington, east across the lake to the Juanita and Kirkland area with the distant

Cliff swallow nests at Magnuson Park

Cascades, and south to the glaciated cone of Mount Rainier. Grass tapers down to water along the shore on either side of the boat launch, and it is possible to plunge in for a swim any place along the shore. However, these areas are unguarded and the water drops off quickly. PWCs landing here can be a hazard. A roped-off swimming area (guarded in summer) is a bit to the north, near a wading pool for toddlers. The beach is only a narrow gravel strip, so it is not ideal for sand play. A swim platform is anchored offshore.

Although much of the park focuses on its waterfront, inland has its attractions, too; sports fields, tennis courts, and a fine hill for flying kites lie at the heart of the peninsula. A long strip along the boundary fence that stretches to the water is an off-leash area where dogs can romp. Pets are required to be leashed elsewhere in the park.

An old maintenance shed beside the shoreline walkway has dozens of mud cliff swallow nests tightly packed under the sheet-metal roof. The birds nest here in spring, then in late summer migrate to wintering grounds as far south as Brazil and Argentina. Undeveloped parts of the park contain four major habitat areas: forest, meadow, shrub/scrub, and shoreline. Here plants and trees are, on their own or with the aid of humans, attempting to return the land to the natural environment that flourished here before the Navy arrived. This range of habitats, each with distinctive plants, attracts an exceptional variety of birds and small animals. A kiosk near the boat launch describes the habitats and tells what birds and animals might be found there. See if you can spot birds such as black-capped chickadees, house finches, or Bullock's orioles.

National Oceanographic and Atmospheric Agency at Sand Point

Facilities: Path, public art

When most of the Sand Point Naval Air Station was surplused, NOAA claimed the peninsula's northern half and converted the former airplane hangers to warehouses. Pontiac Bay is now used for docking and outfitting NOAA research vessels, and new administrative offices have sprung up on shore. Several remarkable government-funded public art installations—some modest, some elaborate—are scattered along the waterfront on a gravel walking path, and a fifth work is inland among the NOAA buildings. The first encountered is an angular footbridge spanning a drainage ditch. Quotes from *Moby Dick,* inset in the surface of this bridge and its companion farther along the path, evoke the ancient sea.

For most visitors, the favorite art installation is slightly east of the path, near the southernmost bridge. Here a grassy hillock holds a number of narrow, 15-foot-high towers topped by antenna-like pipes and metal sheets. As visually interesting as this angular work is, contrasted with the soft natural forms of surrounding land and lake, its greatest beauty lies in the haunting sounds the arrangement makes as breezes blow through it. Eerie tones fill the area, their pitch and volume changing with wind velocity and direction. The title of this installation, *A Sound Garden,* inspired the name of a popular local rock group.

The gravel path continues north along the shore, but a tangle of blackberries and Nootka rose limit beach access. Midway is *Berth Haven,* a spacious patch of grass interrupted by a few low pines leading to a stack

A Sound Garden is a favorite art installation at NOAA.

of wood and metal platforms. The angled water's edge platforms are designed so that waves and boat wakes splash pleasantly over the lower ones. Stop and be lulled by the lake.

Viewpoint, on a grass knoll on the southeast corner of Pontiac Bay, is appropriately named. Several huge tree-shade boulders on a concrete platform have been quarter-sliced, forming a grouping of large basalt seats overlooking the lake—a troll's living room perhaps? Smaller boulders (these uncut) are stacked at water's edge. The entrance road loops around *Knoll for NOAA,* which lies west of the NOAA dock, amid the buildings. It is a contrast of textures on a massive scale, with ivy-covered sides and velvety lawn capped by a smooth concrete dome. Outward-facing benches offer views of the lake.

To reach the beach path, walk through a gate in the fence between Magnuson Park and NOAA or drive into the NOAA Western Regional Center at 7600 Sand Point Way NE. Parking is at the southeast side, near the *A Sound Garden* installation.

Matthews Beach Park (City of Seattle)

Park Area: 20.9 acres
Access: Land
Facilities: Swimming beach (guarded in summer), bathhouse, kitchen shelter, picnic tables (some reservable), barbecues, basketball hoops, children's play equipment, rest rooms

Here is perhaps the quintessential city waterfront park, with one of the nicest swimming areas on Lake Washington, perfect sandy beach, spacious lawns shaded by huge old fir, cedar, hemlock, and maple trees, picnic tables for breaking out the potato chips and burgers, and play areas to turn the kids loose. Its major drawback is that Canada geese think it is nifty, too, so you might have to deal with their mess.

The broad sunny lawn above the beach has ample space to spread a beach towel. Uphill from the bathhouse the grass slope holds scattered shady picnic sites. A broad gully on the north side of this hill has an outdoor single-hoop basketball court and a large children's play area. Another tree-lined picnic area south of the bathhouse fronts on a second beach. The Burke-Gilman Trail skirts the park's west side, so it is a popular resting spot for bicyclists peddling the trail. Because the Burke-Gilman follows the bed of the old SL&E railroad along the lakeshore, this indicates that prior to the lake's lowering in 1916, Matthews Beach was a small watery cove.

The park is the namesake of John G. Matthews, who homesteaded here in the 1880s. A small sawmill operated on the cove's north side in 1894. Matthews Beach also lays claim to a part in Seattle's aviation history. During the 1940s a dock at the south end of what is now the park was

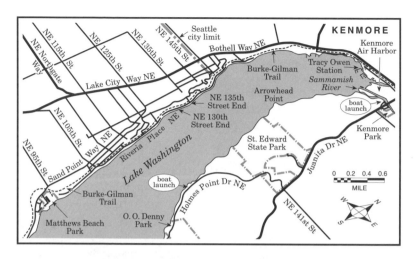

Engineers and underwater explorers at Matthews Beach Park

Tracy Owen Station is a popular stop along the Burke-Gilman Trail.

used by Pan American World Airways "Clipper Ships," the first amphibious transoceanic commercial aircraft.

Thornton Creek cuts through the park's south end, separating the developed portion to the north from a wide, block-long lawn that holds a few benches overlooking the beach. Reach this section of the park by turning off Sand Point Way NE onto Northeast 90th Place; in 1/2 block this street bends north into 51st Avenue NE, which runs along the edge of the park's south section; parking is not permitted along 51st.

The main parking lot is reached by turning off Sand Point Way NE onto Northeast 93rd Street. In 1/2 block a bridge over the creek leads past a Metro pumping station and on into the park. The main park entrance, a short block farther, reaches a pair of large parking lots. Beyond the park entrance, 93rd bends into a stub of 51st Avenue NE; this entire area is reserved for parking for adjoining residences.

Tracy Owen Station (King County)

Park Area: 15.8 acres
Access: Land, water
Facilities: Fishing pier, picnic tables, rest rooms, trail

A testimony to the shallowness of water at the north end of Lake Washington is the huge dock at Tracy Owen Station in Kenmore. This King County park at the lake's northwest corner sports a 630-foot-long concrete dock built when a sawmill operated here. The dock needed to be that long to reach adequate depths for tugs. Finger piers off the dock's end can accommodate up to 20 small craft (day-use only); however, the dock primarily attracts anglers. Swimming is prohibited. Boats of any draft should approach this shoal end of the lake cautiously. A number of old pilings once used for log booming have rotted off just beneath the water surface and are an added hazard. Many are marked with white diamond-shaped warning signs, but these have not been maintained, so there might be underwater surprises for unwary boaters.

South of the mouth of the Sammamish River, the lake channel in the vicinity of the Kenmore Air Harbor has been recently dredged and should present no hazards. The area inside the buoys from the river's mouth to Arrowhead Point is a designated seaplane landing zone where seaplanes have the right-of-way over any boats. Within the zone the boat speed limit is 5 mph.

On-shore amenities at Tracy Owen Station are a few picnic tables found in pleasant grassy pockets along the beach at the head of the dock and south to the park boundary. By far the most popular facility, however, are the rest room and water fountain in the park's center. The park is adjacent to the Burke-Gilman Trail, and this is a favorite stop for bicyclists, joggers, and skaters using the trail. It is also a convenient point to head out on the trail in either direction, so the parking lot is often filled with trail users' vehicles.

A small sand and gravel beach near the rest rooms is within easy wheeling distance of the parking lot, making it a good place to launch and retrieve paddlecraft. With the exception of a few spots of open, low-bank shore at the picnic areas, the remainder of the beach is either narrow marshland or an inaccessible thicket of trees and brush. This shoreline cover provides breeding, feeding, and nesting sites for waterfowl. You might also spot herons, hawks, and even an eagle.

To reach Tracy Owen Station by land, take Bothell Way NE (Highway 522) to the Lake Forest Park/Kenmore vicinity and turn southeast on 61st Avenue NE, which crosses the Burke-Gilman trail. In $1/2$ block the road meets Northeast 175th Street at a T-intersection. The park is $1/2$ block to the west.

THE EAST SHORE

From the mouth of the Sammamish River to Juanita Bay, steep wooded banks, as much as 350 feet high, rise abruptly from narrow beachfront flats. With the exception of two parks—St. Edward State Park and O. O. Denny County Park—and one narrow street end, the shore is completely private.

The largest harbor on Lake Washington lies along the lake's northeast shore—$1/2$-mile wide, nearly round Juanita Bay. The shallow bay faces southwest on the lake, so it is open to storms that sweep up the lake, making it less than ideal for mooring. The first white settlers who arrived on the bay in the 1870s established Hubbard's Landing, a sawmill and shingle mill on its north shore. The community was later renamed Juanita, a name inspired by a popular song of the time. The isolation of the small pioneer community was relieved in 1891 when a corduroy road of

Growth of the Eastside

Instead of the Eastside being the bedroom communities and business parks it is today, it would be a region of factories if things had worked out the way Englishman Peter Kirk planned. In the 1880s the discovery of iron ore near Snoqualmie Pass, the nearby coal mines at Newcastle and Renton, and the huge potential market for steel for railroads in the western U.S., South America, and China prompted Kirk to propose development of a steel mill at Moss Bay, on the east shore of Lake Washington. Construction of blast furnaces and a steel rolling mill began at the site in 1891, and Kirk's land development company built several commercial buildings that would provide the support facilities needed in the new industrial city. A rail spur was laid connecting Kirkland to the newly completed SL&E line that ran around the lake's north end to the Seattle waterfront. This railroad was to be extended to the Snoqualmie Pass mines and also would connect with other short-haul lines from the coal mines to the south.

A major financial panic in 1893 caused markets for steel to collapse, and the railroad was forced into receivership before its tracks reached the mines. In addition, the surface ore deposits at the pass proved to be shallow, and predicted deeper ones were nearly inaccessible. Kirkland's dreams of glory vanished almost overnight, and the "Pittsburgh of the West" instead became a modest agricultural community producing chickens, fruit, and berries. It was one of the terminals for the translake ferry system, and between 1892 and 1927 it was the site of a small woolen mill. Many of the old commercial buildings form the heart of downtown Kirkland today.

logs was extended north from Kirkland and a primitive log bridge crossed Juanita Slough. In the early 1900s Juanita became a popular summer resort area with a long pier providing a landing for boatloads of tourists.

The shore south from Juanita Bay to Yarrow Bay is now all part of Kirkland, although in the past the southern portion of this waterfront was the separate community of Houghton. The beautiful little town is presently struggling with its identity, as there is pressure to permit high-rise apartments and condominiums along its 3-mile-long waterfront. City officials have thus far been able to hold building heights to a modest three to four stories and to keep the older buildings and small shops, along with substantial amounts of public art, that give the city its small-town charm.

Moss Bay, on which Kirkland faces, is a much slighter indentation in the shore than Juanita Bay. However, the protection of Fairweather Point

While Kirkland's dreams of greatness faded, those of Houghton materialized for a time. During the late 1890s heyday of Lake Washington excursion steamers, an entrepreneurial Swedish immigrant, John Anderson, acquired a fleet of steamships that carried recreation seekers between the several amusement parks on the lake's west shore and on outings to Mercer Island and the Eastside. One of these popular destinations was Atlanta Park, just uphill from the Houghton dock. At that time, a small shipyard at Houghton built wooden vessels for service on the lake. Anticipating significant growth in the boat excursion business with the Alaska-Yukon-Pacific Exposition (AYP), Anderson bought the shipyard and enlarged and improved it to meet the demands of his growing fleet. After the AYP closed, Anderson expanded his steamship company to provide ferry and freight service around the lake.

The opening of the locks and ship canal in 1917 made it possible to get newly built ships to saltwater, and a continuous cycle of growth began for the Anderson Shipyard. It built many of the freight and passenger vessels of the Mosquito Fleet that plied Puget Sound, as well as larger ocean-going vessels; it met the World War I demand for ocean-going steamers, employing nearly 400 workers full-time and bringing prosperity to the Eastside. In the 1920s it converted passenger steamers to auto ferries, and in World War II it built and repaired hundreds of Navy vessels. After the war, a nationwide excess of shipbuilding facilities doomed Anderson's shipyards and they shut down. In the late 1980s the prime waterfront the shipyard once occupied was transformed to Carillon Point, an upscale complex with a marina, hotel, restaurant, and stores.

gives it some shelter from storms whipping up Lake Washington. Some anchorages can be had offshore.

St. Edward State Park (State of Washington)

Park Area: 316 acres
Access: Land
Facilities: Group day-use areas, 7 miles of hiking trails, 1 mile of equestrian trail, indoor swimming pool, tennis courts, gymnasium, handball courts, horseshoe pits, sports fields, picnic tables, rest rooms, vault toilets at the beach

A pleasant twist of fate brought about this treasure amid the press of surrounding residential development. St. Edward opened in 1931 as a

Offshore rocks at St. Edward State Park attract swimmers.

Catholic seminary to prepare young men for the priesthood. Because of declining enrollment, it closed in 1976. When Washington State Parks acquired the 300-acre property a year later, the school's collection of beautiful old brick buildings in the heart of the property provided many ready-made recreational facilities: a baseball/soccer field, tennis courts, handball courts, a gymnasium, and an indoor swimming pool. Better yet were spacious lawns for picnicking and cathedral-like second-growth forest where meandering walkways were the only intrusion.

Secluded paths originally used by seminarians for exercise and contemplation have been improved and extended, providing more than 7 miles of trails. In the wooded plateau on the park's north side, between the seminary buildings and Juanita Drive NE, four

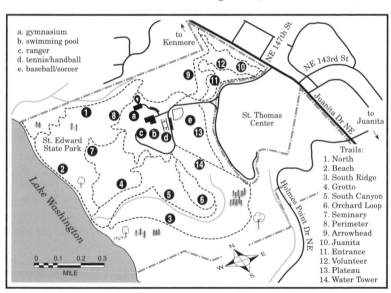

a. gymnasium
b. swimming pool
c. ranger
d. tennis/handball
e. baseball/soccer

to Kenmore

NE 147th St

NE 143rd St

Juanita Dr NE

to Juanita

St. Thomas Center

St. Edward State Park

Lake Washington

Holmes Point Dr NE

Trails:
1. North
2. Beach
3. South Ridge
4. Grotto
5. South Canyon
6. Orchard Loop
7. Seminary
8. Perimeter
9. Arrowhead
10. Juanita
11. Entrance
12. Volunteer
13. Plateau
14. Water Tower

0   0.1   0.2   0.3
MILE

interlinked walkways twine through dense forest. Three additional routes skirt the edges of the park's developed area. All these paths are open to hikers and bicyclists.

Below the seminary complex, the hillside holds a magnificent forest of Douglas-fir, western hemlock, bigleaf maple, and western red cedar with a fill of smaller alder, willow, dogwood, and madrona. Three deep moist ravines with lush growths of ferns and devil's club cut the steep, 300-foot-high bank. Trails descend the ravines to the beach—the North Trail along the park's northern boundary, the Seminary Trail in the park's center, and the Grotto, South Canyon, and South Ridge Trails along the southern perimeter. All are for hikers only, except for the Seminary Trail, which is also open to bicycles. As the dense growth muffles the sounds of civilization, you might well feel you are in the heart of the Cascades, rather than on the shore of an urban lake.

Once at water's level, Beach Trail meanders along the ³/₄-mile-long soft bank above the lake. Here, wind and water have eroded the soft soil, causing trees to topple into the water. These fallen trees provide a secluded cover probed by kayakers exploring the shore. A shallow, gently tapering beach at the foot of the Seminary Trail is a popular spot for wading or swimming. Primitive vault toilets just above the beach also provide a welcome relief spot for hikers or for passing kayakers and canoeists.

To reach St. Edward State Park from the north, drive 68th Avenue SE south from Northeast Bothell Way (Highway 522) and cross the Sammamish River. Here 68th becomes Juanita Drive NE. Continue south for 1.7 miles, then turn west on the road into the park, which is more conspicuously signed for various adjacent addiction recovery centers than for the park itself. Take a road fork to the west to reach the park boundary in 0.4 mile. From the south, take Juanita Drive NE northwest from the junction of Northeast 116th Street and 98th Avenue NE at Juanita Bay Park to arrive at the entrance road in 3.9 miles.

Northeast 130th Place Street End (King County)

Access: Land, water
Facilities: Boat launch ramp

This unobtrusive public street end amid an otherwise unbroken chain of private shoreline residences is the only trailered boat launch between Kirkland and the mouth of the Sammamish River. The 60-foot-wide gravel ramp drops into the lake at the end of Northeast 130th Place. It is available to the public from 8:00 A.M. until sunset; however, as numerous signs make clear, there is no parking for boat trailers anywhere in the vicinity. The nearest public parking area is a gravel lot at O. O. Denny Park, six blocks to the south.

To reach the ramp by land, take Juanita Drive NE south from Kenmore

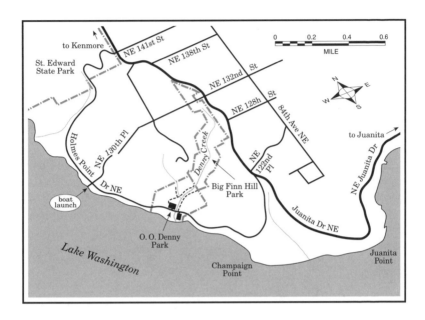

or NE Juanita Drive north from Juanita and turn west onto Holmes Point Drive NE (also marked as 68th Avenue NE at the north end and 76th Place NE at the south end). As the road reaches the beach area, look for the cross street of Northeast 130th Place and the signed public access.

O. O. Denny Park (King County)

Park Area: 46.97 acres
Access: Land, water
Facilities: Picnic tables, barbecues, picnic shelter, hand-carried boat launch, 1.6 miles of trail, rest rooms

Families pouring forth from their minivans will quickly convince you this waterfront picnic spot is well loved. Parents spread a blanket on the grass slopes along the shore and unpack a picnic basket, toddlers splash about on the shallow beach, youngsters explore the mouth of Denny Creek, and teenagers swim and "hang out." Those that own canoes, kayaks, or PWCs beach them here for a day of water sports. Although King County maintains this park, it is owned by the city of Seattle. The property was the country estate of Orion O. Denny, an early Seattleite who donated it to the city in 1922.

The beach is without question the most popular part of the park, but a large chunk of property lies inland on two steep wooded ravines that enclose Denny Creek. A trail on the gravel parking lot's south side connects to Big Finn Hill Park, which follows the Denny Creek drainage northeast for more than 1/2 mile. A second trail on the parking lot's north side traces the opposite side of the drainage uphill for 1/4 mile.

To reach O. O. Denny Park, take Juanita Drive NE south from Kenmore, or north from Juanita, and turn west onto Holmes Point Drive NE (also marked as 68th Avenue NE at the north end and 76th Place NE at the south end). As Holmes Point Drive drops down to follow the lake's shoreline at Holmes Point, it cuts through the park between Northeast 120th and Northeast 124th Streets. A large paved parking lot sits at the south end of the beach section. The lot is within easy paddlecraft-carrying distance of the beach. A gravel lot on the opposite side of Holmes Point Drive holds overflow parking and can be used to park boat trailers using the Northeast 130th Place ramp. Limited parking is also available along Holmes Point Drive, but trailers are not permitted there.

Juanita Beach Park (King County)

Park Area: 25.46 acres
Access: Land, water
Facilities: Swimming beach (guarded in summer), dock, picnic tables, barbecues, picnic shelters, concession stand (in summer), ballfields, tennis courts, children's play equipment, horseshoe pits, outside shower, rest rooms

Juanita Beach Park is everything you would expect of an urban park on prime waterfront, with enough sand for a hundred beach towels to be spread, enough water to satisfy a small village of inflatable-toting youngsters, and enough shaded picnic tables for several delis'-worth of fried chicken and potato salad. In addition, there are ample tennis courts, ballfields, and play equipment to burn off all the excess energy the crowd might generate.

An angled concrete pier wraps around the 800-foot-wide swimming beach—one of the largest on the lake. Families gather here, keeping an eye on toddlers splashing and wading in the shallow inner portion, while swimmers do their laps in deep water. Older kids find the action at the sandy beach on the west side, which is cluttered with bikini-clad sunbathers on summer weekends. Kayaks and PWCs are launched at the shore, and a host of boats of all sizes and descriptions anchor or raft together offshore—party time!

Just inside the entrance, a large parking lot (with speed bumps to control hot rodding) can accommodate about 190 vehicles. However, because of the park's popularity parking spots are hard to come by on summer weekends. On the north side of Northeast Juanita Drive a large grass field is bordered by two tennis courts on the west and baseball diamonds on the north and northeast sides. Parking for this sports area is on the field's east side; rest rooms are near the center of the grassy area.

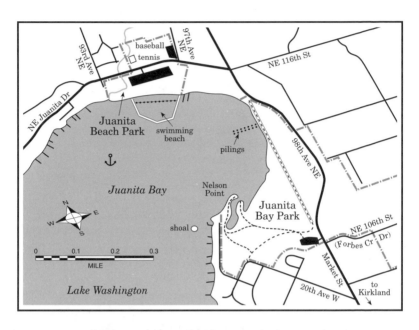

Orca whale sighted at Juanita Beach Park

On cool winter days, when sun-toasted throngs have long since departed, the park, along with others along the Kirkland shore, is a fine spot to commune with gulls and enjoy invigorating wind-driven lake spray.

To reach the park, take the Northeast 85th Street exit from Highway 405, head west to the center of Kirkland, and then go north on Market Street. Alternatively, take the Northeast 124th Street exit, follow 124th west to 100th Avenue NE, and turn south on it. Either route will lead you to the intersection of 98th Avenue NE and Northeast Juanita Drive; the park is two blocks west.

Juanita Bay Park (City of Kirkland)

Park Area: 113 acres
Access: Land
Facilities: Picnic tables, benches, causeway, boardwalks, trails, interpretive displays, rest rooms

At times, nature has a way of resisting man's most determined efforts to tame or "improve" it. Wetlands are a fine example of this, often continuing to seep and sag despite all the filling and smoothing bulldozers might do. If we're lucky, the land hasn't been irretrievably damaged before we see the light and let Mom Nature have her way. Juanita Bay Park at Nelson Point is one place where nature has triumphed—at least partially. The wetlands on the south side of Juanita Bay originally were spawning grounds for salmon and home to muskrat, beaver, otter, deer, and waterfowl. Members of a local Sammamish tribe lived here, harvesting the abundant fish and wildlife. Marsh plants provided them with berries and materials for weaving mats, baskets, and clothing.

In 1891 Dorr Forbes built a plank bridge across the bog to connect with a rough road from Kirkland. When the lake was lowered by the opening of the ship canal in 1916, the steamer dock on Juanita Bay became unusable, and a part of the original wetlands dried. With the habitat dwindling, the fish and wildlife died or departed, causing the remaining Native American population to move away.

By the early 1920s the rich bottomland of the former marsh was used for truck gardening, and the remaining wetland, Forbes Creek Slough, was used to raise frogs for frog legs to be served in Seattle's gourmet restaurants. In 1927 construction began on a golf course that had been planned since 1910. Over the next six years tons of cedar bark, sawdust, and fill dirt were dumped into the site. A new bridge was built across the slough in 1932, and the nine-hole golf course at Nelson Point opened a year later. However, despite the construction of berms and pumping, the fairways and greens on the golf course's north side settled slowly into old marshland. The course became impractical to maintain, and closed in 1975—nature had won.

Purple loosestrife grows on pilings from the old steamer dock at Juanita Bay.

The city of Kirkland purchased the golf course property for a park and converted the old 1932 bridge, which had been replaced by a wider span, to an elevated interpretive walkway along the bay's east shore. Signs on the bridge railings tell the story of the marshland. Portions of the golf course that have been reclaimed by the marsh now hold the East and West Boardwalk Nature Trails, which also have interpretive signs. Uphill to the south, drier slopes of the old fairways are still framed by lovely old willows, Douglas-firs, and poplars. Paved paths with benches and picnic tables scattered along them lead from here to the nature trails.

The entrance to the park is west of the intersection of Market Street and Forbes Creek Drive (Northeast 106th Street). A parking lot here has space for 30 cars. No parking is available in Juanita at the north end of the old slough bridge.

Kiwanis Park (City of Kirkland)

Park Area: 1.9 acres
Access: Land, water
Facilities: Walking path

This undeveloped section of Lake Washington waterfront is little more than a steep wooded hillside above a 500-foot strip of shoreline. A graveled path leads down from the street to a muddy path along the water's edge. Several large maple, alder, and willows line the beach, but a few breaks in the foliage offer low-bank access to the water and the gradually sloping cobble beach. The upland bank, which is thickly wooded and has

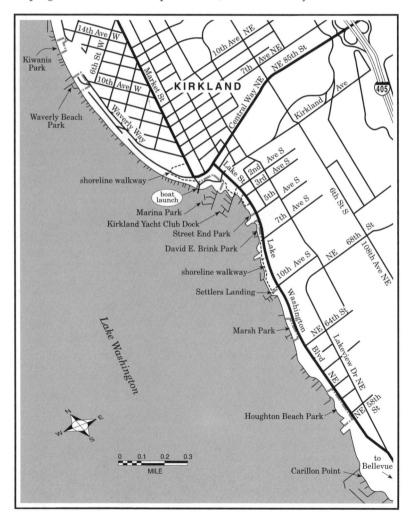

a dense cover of blackberries, is steep enough to make the beach trail too difficult for hand-carrying boats for launching, but boats launched elsewhere can easily land here for leg stretching.

To reach the park, take Market Street north from Kirkland to 16th Avenue W. Drive northwest on 16th for three blocks, then turn southwest on 8th Avenue W, which in a block bends north, becomes 14th Avenue W for about 50 feet, and then curves north more to become 10th Avenue W. The park, unmarked except for a sign indicating hours of use, is below the street at this point. Parking for a few cars is available on either side of the street.

Waverly Beach Park (City of Kirkland)

Park Area: 2.8 acres
Access: Land, water
Facilities: Swimming beach (guarded in summer), dock, picnic tables, children's play equipment, rest rooms

This cozy little park tucked into the bluffs north of Kirkland is certainly not the largest or grandest on the lake, but it has one of the nicest swimming beaches. The area, enclosed by a wooden dock, has all the advantages of a protected swimming pool, with the added joys of a sandy bottom

Fishing draws all ages to Waverly Beach Park.

and invigorating lake water. Low concrete steps leading into the water let tots cool their toes in shallow water.

A 200-foot-long dock with a small T-shaped end has a planked step along its north side that is low enough for paddlecraft and sailboards to be launched. Motorized craft are not permitted to approach the dock. North of the dock, the railing above a 3-foot-high concrete bulkhead holds a pair of built-in table/benches for shoreside anglers. This is said to be one of the best places on the lake for trout. Tall old trees on shore above the swim area shade a swing set and a lawn sporting a few picnic tables. Stairs along the park's south boundary climb from the beach up to Waverly Way.

To reach the park from downtown Kirkland, take Market Street north and in one block head northwest on Waverly Way. The park entrance is at Waverly Way and 6th Street W; a narrow road threads down the bank to a parking lot at the park's north end with room for about 20 cars. A second lot halfway up the slope can hold another 30 cars, but parking is at a premium on warm summer days, and streetside parking is not permitted along Waverly Way in the vicinity.

Marina Park (City of Kirkland)

Park Area: 2.5 acres
Access: Land, water
Facilities: Dock, guest moorage, boat launch ramp, rest rooms, picnic tables, picnic shelter, public art, tour boats

The Kirkland waterfront on Moss Bay has been an Eastside water transportation hub since the early 1900s when it served as a terminal for the county's Lake Washington ferry system. Although the completion of the first Lake Washington floating bridge in 1940 spelled the end of the ferries, the waterfront continued to embody the soul of the community. Marina Park in Kirkland is the place to bring your boat to visit the town, or it's the place to hang out and watch boats. This is one of two places on Lake Washington that offers overnight guest moorage (the other is Gene Coulon Memorial Park, in Renton). The city operates a tour boat dock at the old ferry terminal site in Marina Park, along with the Port of Seattle, which joined in the effort in order to relieve some of the pressure of tourist activities on the Seattle waterfront. Kirkland's water-oriented restaurants, shops, and other attractions are a short stroll away.

North of the moorage area, a small sand and pea-gravel beach is studded with granite boulders and huge driftwood logs. A semicircle of low steps rimming the shore is a fine place to sun while keeping an eye on youngsters scrambling on the boulders and dabbling in the water. A lawn above the beach holds picnic tables, benches, rest rooms, and some shade trees. A tall, multilevel fountain pleasantly trickles water; on a knoll above, a bronze sculpture portrays animated children holding hands as they leap a puddle—having just as much fun as the real-life children playing around them. At the park's northwest side, a large roofed pavilion serves as a group picnic shelter and meeting place.

A single-lane public boat launch with an adjoining boarding float lies on the park's north edge. Use of the launch ramp is free and unrestricted from November to March; for the remainder of the year, users must purchase a pass card. Access to the ramp is on a first-come, first-served basis; a two-lane waiting area runs along Market Street in the block north of Central Way NE. Parking for cars and trailers is available in gravel lots at the ends of Waverly Park, northwest of the intersection of Market Street and Waverly Way, and along Waverly Way.

Kirkland Yacht Club Marina Dock (City of Kirkland)
Access: Land, water
Facilities: Dock

A large private marina complex south of Marina Park has a 250-foot-long dock extending out from the shore with several gated finger piers off its north side. The main dock, as well as the moorage along its south side, are open to the public, but overnight moorage is not permitted. Two restaurants sit at the dock's shore end, and the heart of Kirkland with small shops and more eateries is just two blocks away.

As of the summer of 1997 the old fireboat *Duwamish* was moored here and was available for informal tours on weekends when volunteers were

The fireboat Duwamish *at Kirkland*

aboard working on restoration projects. The vessel, the largest municipal fireboat in the world, was retired from service in 1984. The nonprofit group restoring it hopes to return it to standby active service on Lake Washington and Lake Union. It will also serve as a historic tourist attraction. The vessel might be moved to Lake Union in the future if negations with government agencies makes a site there available.

Kirkland Shoreline Pedestrian Walkways
(City of Kirkland)
Access: Land

In addition to Kirkland's generous supply of parks on Moss Bay, the city has several blocks'-worth of paved public walkways along the waterfront just above the beach, offering fine lake views. Docks along the paths are private, as are abutting apartment and condominium complexes inland. The pathways are marked by posts and descriptive plaques where they join nearby thoroughfares.

From north to south, the walkways are (1) along the block of beach between the north side of the Marina Park launch ramp at Market Street and the 100 block of Lake Street W, (2) between the Kirkland Yacht Club Marina, at the end of 2nd Avenue S and Kirkland Marina Park, (3) along the block of beach off Lake Street between 3rd and 4th Avenue S, and (4) along the beach between 10th Avenue S and 7th Avenue S, with an intermediate access at 8th Avenue S.

Street End Park **(City of Kirkland)**
Park Area: 0.02 acre
Access: Land

Tersely descriptive, Street End Park is just that—a 50-foot-wide chunk of shoreline at the end of 5th Avenue S, west of Lake Street. A concrete deck has a lone bench surrounded by planters with posies and bushes. Lake views are sandwiched between the walls of condos on adjoining properties.

David E. Brink Park **(City of Kirkland)**
Park Area: 1.15 acres
Access: Land
Facilities: Dock, public art, *disabled access*

A steep grass slope drops to a shoreline that weaves gracefully along this three-block-long section of Kirkland waterfront. The park's treeless south end has a concrete path that gradually switchbacks from street level to the beach, providing easy disabled access.

In the middle of the park a 20-foot high platform, topped with a deck and benches, overlooks the water and park activity. Below, a 150-foot-long wooden dock ends in a narrow T-shaped platform with benches that are ideal for fishing or sunbathing. Low concrete steps south of the dock offer wading (or unguarded swimming) in cool lake water.

The grass bank, edged by Lake Washington Boulevard NE sweeps north for 2 blocks; walk the shore, duck under ancient willows, and gander at geese. At street level, a bronze sculpture, the *Water Bearers,* shows Native American women gathered around a small pool.

Settlers Landing (City of Kirkland)
Park Area: 0.3 acre
Access: Land
Facilities: Dock, pedestrian walkway

At the end of 10th Avenue S a section of pedestrian walkway, edged by a 40-foot-wide band of grass, connects Lake Washington Boulevard NE and a long street-end dock. Finger piers along the dock's south side are gated and private; however, the dock itself and an L-extension to the north at its end are public. Moorage is short-term day use only, restricted to 30 minutes—enough time to drop in by boat to stretch your legs or walk a block up 10th to a deli. The dock's end offers anglers a chance for salmon or some of the other fish lurking in lake waters below.

Marsh Park (City of Kirkland)
Park Area: 2.6 acres
Access: Land, water
Facilities: Dock, picnic tables, hand-carried boat launch, rest rooms

Perhaps this park is named for a marsh that once existed here, or maybe for a Mr. Marsh. Whatever the reason for the name, it's a dandy spot to drop in hand-carried boats to investigate inlets and marshes to the south. A deck and a dock are the major features of the little park. The concrete deck at the center of the park holds tree-shaded benches and tables. A spacious open lawn at the park's south side offers ample toasting room for summer sunbathers; at its north side, large old trees spread over the tiered grass slope.

The low-bank, boulder bulkhead stretching along the 200-foot-long section of Kirkland waterfront is interrupted by a 100-foot-long fishing dock and a strip of gravel beach. Carry paddlecraft the short distance from the small parking lot for launching. Swimming is permitted here, but the beach is not guarded.

Find the park below Lake Washington Boulevard NE, north of Northeast 66th Place.

Houghton Beach Park (City of Kirkland)

Park Area: 0.5 acre
Access: Land, water
Facilities: Swimming beach (guarded in summer), dock, hand-carried boat launch, picnic tables, children's play equipment, rest rooms

The close-cropped green lawn of Kirkland's Houghton Beach Park lies below Lake Washington Boulevard NE, along a three-block-long section between Northeast 58th and Northeast 61st Streets. A small parking lot at the park's south end accommodates about 20 cars; a second small vehicle access at the center of the park has only load/unload space. Additional parking is on adjoining side streets.

Rest rooms and children's play equipment hold forth in the park's midsection. Below them, a 100-yard-long dock has a near-shore jog that protects the shallow portion of the swimming area. An offshore swim float and a line of floats between it and the dock outline the designated swimming area, guarded during summer months. The short L-section at the dock's north end attracts anglers. Another open grass plot north of the swimming beach has a sand deck for volleyball—bring your own standards and net. The park's north side is edged by a waterfront restaurant; the dock there is for the use of patrons arriving by boat.

Gentle sand and gravel beaches at the park's center and south end are ideal for launch and retrieval of canoes and kayaks. Wetlands at the head of Yarrow Bay lie only a short paddle to the south.

Launching kayaks at Houghton Beach Park

Carillon Point

Access: Land, water
Facilities: Restaurants, hotel, shops, day-use moorage, private marina

Once the site of the Anderson Shipyard, this prime strip of Lake Washington shoreline was rebuilt in the 1990s as upscale Carillon Point. A beachfront hotel, restaurants, office buildings, and trendy shops surround a brick pavilion at the heart of the complex.

A large private marina occupies the harbor where steamers once were launched. The breakwater along the marina's north and west sides is available as public moorage (two-hour limit) for visiting boaters. Plaques along the waterfront path tell of the excursion boats that once plied the lake in the late 1890s and relate the history of the shipyard that occupied the shoreline here for more than 60 years. Try to imagine the bustling, grimy industrial business that once filled this area—or the Seattle Seahawks' training camp that was here more recently.

YARROW BAY, COZY COVE, AND FAIRWEATHER BAY

Lying between Carillon Point and the Evergreen Point Bridge, within a hubcap's toss of the busy Highway 520 freeway, three large coves bracketed by fingers of land offer boaters anchorages ranging from pretty good

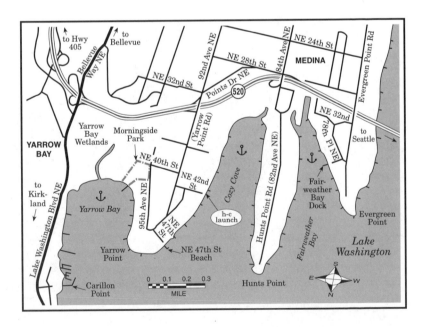

to exquisite. The easternmost inlet, Yarrow Bay, has 20 feet of water at its entrance, but it quickly rises to depths of 10 feet or less. At the head of the rounded bay is a 100-acre wetland, home to a wealth of birds and small mammals, which has survived the threat of commercial development. Separating Yarrow Bay and Cozy Cove is the heavily residential peninsula of Yarrow Point.

Cozy Cove, the 1-mile-deep indentation of Lake Washington between Yarrow Point and Hunts Point, is sheltered from weather except from the north (which generally is the direction of fair-weather winds, anyway). The soft muddy bottom, ranging from 10 to 40 feet deep, offers a solid anchorage from which to enjoy water views that cost shoreside residents somewhere in the million-dollar range—a pretty good bargain! Beach property at Hunts Point, on the west side of Cozy Cove, is even more exclusive than that on Yarrow Point; there are no public shoreline accesses within the community.

Fairweather Bay, the 3/4-mile-long northwest-oriented bay between Hunts Point and Evergreen Point, is a somewhat less desirable moorage than Cozy Cove. Water depths in the bay range from 4 to 20 feet, so the anchorage is not suitable for boats of substantial draft, and the bay's broad mouth is subject to more wind and chop than the deeper Cozy Cove. Evergreen Point, the westernmost of the three fingers of land, is a part of the town of Medina.

Yarrow Bay Wetlands (City of Kirkland)
Park Area: 66 acres
Access: Boat

Improbably tucked between the posh residences of Yarrow Point and spanking-new commercial developments of south Kirkland, the Yarrow Bay Wetlands seem miles and decades distant from both. Dense marsh growths of willows, reeds, cattails, irises, and water lilies rise from the ooze to form a sensory barrier against the surrounding civilization that not even the incessant roar of traffic on nearby Highway 520 can diminish.

A shallow channel, barely kayak deep, penetrates this minuscule wilderness for nearly 1/4 mile, passing shoreside beaver dams, mama ducks herding tiny puffballs fresh from the nest, and statuelike herons assessing the intentions of intruders. In the top of a tree snag a bald eagle sits, contemplating a lunch of the Pomeranian strolling the nearby Carillon Point mall. Swifts dart along the channel's surface swooping up bugs.

All this is but a short paddle from downtown Kirkland. The nearest public launch point is at Houghton Beach Park, but the wetlands are within easy reach of any of the city's shorefront parks where hand-carried boats may also be put in. Move slowly, spend an hour or an afternoon, and savor the profusion of bog plants and wildlife.

A kayaker discovers a beaver lodge in the Yarrrow Bay Wetlands.

Morningside Park (Town of Yarrow Point)

Access: Land

This dense marshland forest along the southwest side of the Yarrow Bay Wetlands once had primitive trails carved down the steep hillside into the bay's wetlands. The rapid and relentless natural growth outpaced the community's limited maintenance efforts, and the park below the east side of the town hall is now impenetrable. If you wish to try brush beating to find the abandoned paths, take 92nd Avenue NE (Yarrow Point Road) north from Highway 520 to Northeast 40th (Yawata) Street, then head north on 95th Avenue NE (Bonny Brae Drive) for ½ block to the parking lot at the town hall. Consider reestablishing the trails as a conservation club project.

Northeast 47th Street Beach (Town of Yarrow Point)

Access: Land
Facilities: Dock, swimming beach (unguarded), *disabled access*

The town of Yarrow Point transformed this street end on Cozy Cove to create a beautiful neighborhood park for swimming, sunbathing, or just enjoying a whiff of lake air. From the end of Northeast 47th Street (Hayden Way), the beach is accessible by both stairs and a gentle ramp that weaves down the landscaped bank. A 20-foot-wide grass bowl reaches down to a low rock bulkhead above a gradually tapering sand and gravel swimming beach. A 160-foot-long dock with attached swim ladders extends into the bay from the beach's north side. At the dock's end a wood-planked platform holds a pair of benches overlooking Cozy Cove.

An idyllic spot indeed, with one drawback—there is no parking near the beach except for the two spots at the street end for disabled persons. The nearest public parking is two blocks to the east along 92nd Avenue NE (Yarrow Point Road), and even this space is limited to a few cars.

Northeast 42nd Street End (Town of Yarrow Point)
Access: Land, water
Facilities: Hand-carried boat launch ramp

A second public access to the east shore of Cozy Cove is located at the end of Northeast 42nd Street (Loch Lane), two blocks west of 92nd Avenue NE (Yarrow Point Road). Here an unimproved, 20-foot-wide, 100-foot-long swath of grass leads down to a gently sloping concrete ramp with a small, low boarding step alongside. This would be a dandy place to put in boats for long paddles around the nearby inlets, but parking is a problem here also. It is prohibited at the street end; the nearest parking is some limited streetside space a block away on 91st Avenue NE (Sunnyside Street) or two blocks away along 92nd.

Fairweather Bay Dock (Town of Medina)
Access: Land, water
Facilities: Dock

This little-known Medina public dock on the west shore of Fairweather Bay is difficult to find from either land or water (probably to the great relief of neighboring property owners). By water, look for a 175-foot-long dock with a prominent rectangular platform and a swim float on the end, midway along the bay's west side. It is the longest dock in the vicinity. This is one of the few places along this section of shore where paddlers can stop for a break.

To reach the dock by land, take the 84th Avenue NE exit from Highway 520 and then head south to Northeast 24th Street. Here turn west, and at a T-intersection in several blocks, head north on Evergreen Point Road. In 0.7 mile turn east on 78th Place NE. In about one block, where 78th Place bends to the south, look for a narrow paved road to the east, unmarked Lake Lane in the 3400 block of 78th Place NE. The single-lane road leads east for about two blocks past private driveways, then ends in a short gravel drive leading to a Metro pumping station. The dock is at the end of the tree-lined path east from here. Parking is not available below 78th.

CHAPTER FOUR

THE SAMMAMISH RIVER AND LAKE SAMMAMISH

THE SAMMAMISH RIVER

The Sammamish River flows north from the end of Lake Sammamish, then midway along its course turns west to drain into Lake Washington, following a gully left by an ancient glacier. The 14-mile-long watercourse runs between steep banks, ranging from 3 feet to over 10 feet high. These banks, which are reminders of the time when the river was much deeper, before Lake Washington was lowered, give boaters some shelter from wind.

Except for a few weeks during spring run-off, the river is placid, and the current is insignificant for boat travel in either direction. It runs fastest in a 100-yard stretch bordering Marymoor Park, where the water exits from Lake Sammamish, although even here it is easy enough for novice paddlers to handle. Powerboats are permitted in the river (the speed limit is 5 mph); however, a low weir about the middle of the west side of Marymoor Park has only enough clearance for paddlecraft.

The downriver stretch of the river between its mouth and Woodinville still has many of the lazy, twisting elbows of the original watercourse; here new marshland

Opposite: *Racing sculls work out in the Sammamish River near Marymoor Park.* Above right: *Boating on the Sammamish River.*

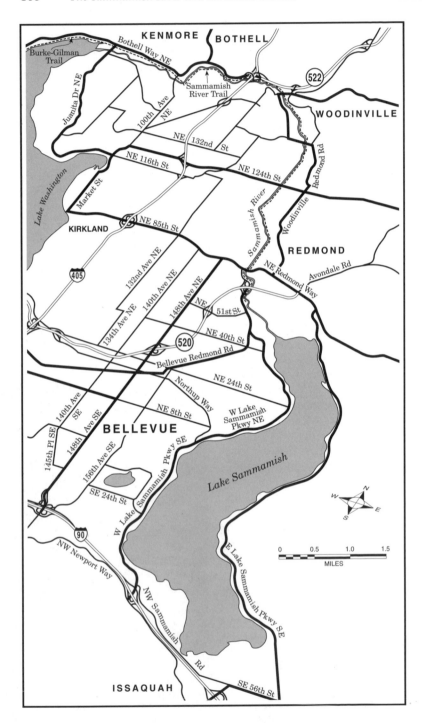

grasses and flowers, waterfowl, and overhead-circling raptors are discovered around each bend as you leisurely paddle or boat. Powerboat use increases as the mouth of the river is neared, making it less attractive for paddlers. The channel is quite shallow near the river's end, so boats of any draft must use caution.

If boating gets boring, toss a fishline overboard to see what you can haul in. The river offers fine fishing from either bank or boat. Winter steelhead are caught here, as well as sea-run cutthroat in spring and fall. Trout are catch-and-release only. Other fish such as catfish or crappie might be hooked.

68th Avenue NE Launch Ramp
(Washington Department of Wildlife)
Park Area: 5 acres
Access: Land, water
Facilities: Boat launch ramp, vault toilets

This Spartan launch ramp provided by the Washington Department of Wildlife is the only such facility near the north end of Lake Washington. The single-lane concrete ramp, actually located on the Sammamish River near its mouth, is fronted by a large gravel parking lot with room for about 25 cars and trailers. Hand-carried boats don't need the ramp to launch here, as the boulder bulkhead along the remainder of the beach is low enough to permit putting them in with no difficulty. No fee is charged for launching, but persons using the area must possess a current hunting, fishing, or conservation license.

Launching at the 68th Avenue NE ramp

Squak to Sammamish, Slough to River

Forests of huge trees brought early pioneers to the Puget Sound region, but by the 1880s the shores in the Seattle vicinity were cleared and that area became civilized. Settlers pushed eastward into the unlogged expanses of Lake Washington and the Squak and Sammamish Valleys. Among these enterprising pioneers were Ira Woodin, David Bothell, John Blyth, and George Brackett.

In early days the Squak River (which was to become the Sammamish) followed a serpentine route, framed by a jungle of vegetation broken only by a few pioneer settlements. Cut timber was boomed and rafted down Lake Sammamish, the Squak River, and Lake Washington, then shot through a flume to Lake Union to reach mills at the lake's south end. Debris and other navigational hazards were cleared from the river to allow steamers to regularly travel from Lake Sammamish to Lake Washington, with intermediate whistle-stops at Redmond, Woodinville, and Bothell to pick up passengers and freight. Farms on the rich bottomland south of Lake Sammamish shipped produce to Seattle markets by canoe or small boat on a circuitous route down the lake and river, and then down Lake Washington.

By the end of the 1880s shingle mills and sawmills had been set up along the banks of the Squak River, and steamers and barges hauled sawed lumber to Seattle for transfer to ships headed for distant markets. (Much of the lumber for the building of San Francisco, and its rebuilding after the 1906 earthquake, came from the Puget Sound region.) Coal deposits found near Issaquah were shipped in small quantities via the same route. The growing communities along the route prospered on the steamer and scow traffic. The 1887 arrival of the SL&E rail line was an even greater boon to these towns, which became freight depots on the new transportation line. Arrival of the railroad also spelled growth for the Lake Sammamish area, which was now able to economically exploit its coal and timber resources, as well as ship the products of its growing dairy and poultry farms.

The lowering of Lake Washington in 1916 spelled the end for most of the steamers plying the Squak River—the channel was now too shallow. As harvestable timber disappeared from the Squak Valley, logged-off tracts became farms and dairies, supplying milk, rabbits, chickens, fruit, and vegetables to Seattle tables. Unfortunately, the docile slough regularly became a menace, surging over its banks and inundating farmland when swollen by spring rain and mountain snowmelt. To end this flooding and stabilize the farming industry, the river was straightened and dredged in the early 1900s. If this were not environmental outrage enough, to protect more acreage from annual flooding it was further straightened in the 1960s (when people should have known better). This tamed channel was known as the Sammamish Slough, and later it was renamed the Sammamish River.

The 20-mile-long river became the 14-mile-long version you see today; the Holsteins and Rhode Island Reds were safe, but some 20,000 acres of wetland habitat was destroyed. Diverting side streams into culverts prevented salmon from reaching tributary spawning creeks, cutting riverbank shade trees caused the water to become too warm for spawning in the Sammamish, removing submerged roots and logs eliminated hiding places for fish, and clearing trees and shrubs along the river destroyed cover for birds, amphibians, and other wildlife. Finally, the disaster has been recognized and steps are being taken to fix it, although it will never be the environmental treasure it once was. The Sammamish Restoration Project is actively working at reopening channels that had been closed over, replacing the vegetation, and putting protective debris back in the water. Plans call for some of the bends to be put back into the channel.

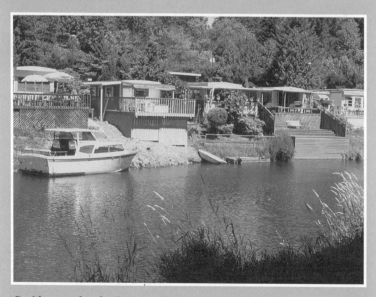

Residences edge the Sammamish River east of Bothell.

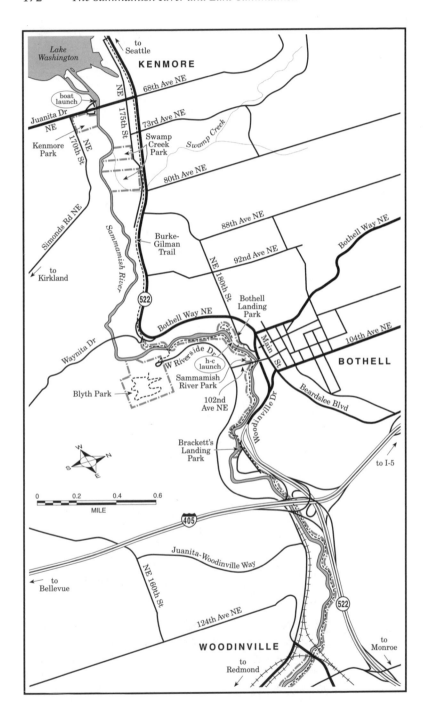

The entrances to the launch ramp, about halfway between the Sammamish River and Simonds Road NE, are poorly marked, so you need to keep a sharp eye out for them if you do not know the area. Southbound traffic can turn directly into the parking lot. (Make sure you are in the right-hand lane as you cross the bridge.) A median concrete barrier on 68th Avenue NE between Northeast 174th Street and Simonds Road NE makes it impossible for northbound traffic to turn left into the area. Northbound traffic should take the unmarked road about 200 yards north of Simonds Road; it circles back under a low bridge (9-foot clearance) to the ramp parking lot.

Kenmore Park (King County)

Park Area: 12.5 acres
Access: Land
Facilities: Picnic tables, picnic shelters, children's play equipment, rhododendron garden, rest rooms

May is the time to visit this small park on the south bank of the Sammamish River. It is then that the exquisite rhododendron gardens are a blazing mass of blossoms—you'll marvel at the many sizes, colors, and kinds. Even when the rhodies aren't busting out, the park is ideal for family or small group picnics. Two brick picnic shelters linked by a walkway are surrounded by shallow pools, large Douglas-fir and cedar, and ever-present rhododendrons. A circular grass area adjoining the shelters has a couple of standards for a volleyball net (you provide). The heart of the park, also surrounded by gardens, is a large grass field with a few more picnic tables and a children's play area.

Although the park fronts on the Sammamish River, there is no practical river access, as a dense swamp separates the main property from the river. A few paths have been beaten into the head-high grass and rushes, but they become quite soggy underfoot before reaching more than glimpses of the river.

To reach the park, take 68th Avenue NE south from Bothell Way NE to Simonds Road NE, or from the south, take Juanita Drive NE, which 68th becomes south of this intersection. Turn east on Simonds Road, and in one block, at 70th Avenue NE, turn north into the park. The parking lot is just inside the entrance.

Swamp Creek Park (King County)

Park Area: 28.4 acres
Access: Land, water

Although Swamp Creek Park fronts on the north shore of the Sammamish River, the property is an undeveloped open space. Two beaten paths lead through the trees and thick brush to a riverside marsh, but both become sodden and impassable about 200 feet from the riverbank. The park property is located on the south side of the 7500 block of Northeast 175th Street, about three blocks east of 73rd Avenue NE.

The Burke-Gilman and Sammamish River Trails

(King County)
Park Area: 346.5 acres
Access: Land, water
Facilities: (Burke-Gilman Trail) 2 miles of multi-use trail; (**Sammamish River Trail**) 9.6 miles of multi-use trail, 6 miles of equestrian trail, benches, picnic tables

From Kenmore's Tracy Owen Station, the Burke-Gilman Trail parallels the south side of Bothell Way NE, following the old railroad route for 2 miles. At 94th Avenue NE the 6-foot-wide strip of asphalt ducks through an underpass and seamlessly joins the Sammamish River Trail in Bothell, 17³/₄ miles away from its beginning in the heart of Ballard. It is hoped that in the near future, once the legal hassles for this rail-trail conversion are resolved, the Sammamish River Trail's south end will connect with the East Lake Sammamish Trail, making a 40-mile-long grand promenade all the way from Shilshole Bay to Issaquah, and offering body-building and mind-freeing recreation to people throughout the region.

The Sammamish River Trail, much loved by walkers, joggers, tricylists, bicyclists, and skaters (as well as blackberry pickers), is actually a combination of a paved path that follows the Sammamish River bank between Bothell and Marymoor Park and several other unpaved side trails either adjacent to the main trail or across the river from it. The trail has become a source of pride for Eastsiders; both Woodinville and Redmond are planning fine parks that will enhance it.

Beginning on the west side of the Sammamish River, across from Blyth Park, the path passes by an old railroad trestle, then drops down to the riverbank and crosses the river on a footbridge. It remains on the river's east or south bank to about Northeast 176th Street. Here it recrosses on another footbridge, reaching the north bank a block west of Brackett's Landing Park. The paved trail remains on this side of the river for the next 8 miles, then a third footbridge at Leary Way NE in Redmond carries the path to the west bank again, where it continues the remaining ¹/₂ mile to Marymoor Park.

Numerous points along the route where it passes through parks, or where it is crossed by roads, provide access. Rest rooms are in many of the parks and along the trail near Northeast 145th and Northeast 116th Streets. Between Bothell and Woodinville occasional trailside pockets of grass hold either a picnic table, bench, or exercise station. In sections of the trail

Bicyclists on the Sammamish River Trail south of Woodinville

between Woodinville and Redmond, the right-of-way inland from the river is wide enough for a parallel dirt equestrian path.

The county also owns portions of the river's west bank between Woodinville and Redmond; the section of the bank between Northeast 116th Street and Northeast 85th Street has a dirt path along the river's edge that is accessible from a few intersecting streets.

Recognition of the massive negative impact previous flood-control measures have had led to a major habitat restoration project in this stretch of the river. A new channel to the Woodin Creek tributary has opened access to spawning grounds. The banks north of Northeast 124th Street have been terraced and planted with trees and shrubs, and submerged log deflectors and shoreline debris have been introduced in this stretch of the river. The stream entering the river at Powerline Crossing south of Northeast 116th Street has been restored to provide an inflow of fresh cool water. With time we might see if man's restoration efforts are as effective as his destructive capabilities.

Bothell Landing Park (City of Bothell)

Park Area: 13 acres
Access: Land, water
Facilities: Picnic tables, children's play equipment, historical museum, hand-carried boat launch, amphitheater, wetlands trail, multi-use trail, rest rooms, *disabled access*

As the Sammamish River Trail follows the old SL&E railbed along the Sammamish River's east bank southwest of Bothell it arrives at a wood footbridge that gracefully arches over the river. On the opposite side is history-rich Bothell Landing Park. The three old buildings on the river's west bank have all been brought here from their previous locations to preserve them. The Lytle House, built in the 1890s by Bothell's doctor, now houses the Northshore Adult Day Center. The Hannen House next door, which dates from 1893, is now the Bothell Historical Museum (open from 1:00 P.M. to 4:00 P.M. on Sundays). Nearby is the 1884 Beckstrom Log Cabin. The community school bell, once used to summon residents for significant events, hangs in an adjacent gazebo. At one time a tiny cove was dredged into the shore south of the bridge; it was rimmed with brick steps to form an amphitheater, and a small performance dock was placed in the cove's center. The deteriorating dock was removed in 1997, and

A walker pauses on the bridge between Bothell Landing Park and Sammamish River Park.

the city is in the process of filling in the cove to restore the original riverbank. Plans are for the amphitheater to be retained; a new performance stage on the landfill will be used for summer concerts.

At the park's south end a paved path leads to the paddlecraft launch area on a sand-filled bank above a low timber bulkhead. This is an ideal spot to launch or retrieve hand-carried craft for exploring the north end of the Sammamish River.

Just beyond the ramp is the start of Wetland Trail, a boardwalk loop through a tiny bog centered around a marsh pond. Interpretive panels along the path recount the geological history of the wetland's development, the critical pollution-filtering function it performs, and the habitat for birds and wildlife that it provides. A picnic table at the loop's far south end is a fine spot to break out the snacks and enjoy the sounds of river and marsh. An enclosed case next to the river holds a narrow, 13-foot-long dugout canoe (small by standards of the day) once used by settlers to travel the river. A nearby panel tells of the river's recreational uses over time.

To reach Bothell Landing Park by land, turn east from Highway 522 (Bothell Way NE) onto Northeast 180th Street, 0.2 mile southwest of the intersection of 522 and Main Street in the heart of Bothell. A small lot lies at the park's west side, and a larger gravel lot is north of the road at the park's east end.

Blyth Park (City of Bothell)

Park Area: 30 acres
Access: Land, water
Facilities: Picnic tables, picnic shelters (reservable), rest rooms, volleyball court, sand pit play area, hiking trails, *disabled access*

Pioneer John Blyth, who arrived in the area in the late 1870s, cleared large sections of land on the Sammamish River's east side, south of Bothell. This pleasant family-oriented park named for him lies just east of his homestead. At the heart of the park, on a high bluff above the river's east bank, are broad green meadows with a pair of picnic shelters, a host of picnic tables shaded by large old cedars, rest rooms, and an elaborate children's play area. A volleyball court on the lawn adjacent to the picnic area is large enough to invite other impromptu team games.

To the west, the lawn drops steeply to the Sammamish River where a low bank and a wooden bulkhead offer easy spots for passing river paddlers to land their boats and take advantage of the park rest rooms and picnic tables. However, the long haul from the parking lot and the steepness of the grass bank make this a difficult put-in site. By water, the park is southwest of Bothell, about 100 yards south of the railroad trestle crossing the river.

Picnicking at Blyth Park

The woods on the park's east side is dense second-growth fir, alder, cedar, and maple with an understory of sword fern, Oregon grape, and thorny berry bushes. A ³/₄-mile-long loop trail weaving through these woods offers a cool secluded respite from the sunny sports fields. Trailside blackberry bushes hold tasty delights in August. A spur trail runs from the park's entrance to the Sammamish River Trail, joining it at the east end of a footbridge crossing the river.

To reach the park, leave Highway 522 at the intersection with Main Street in Bothell and follow Main east for two blocks to the intersection with 102nd Avenue NE. Turn south on 102nd, cross over the highway and the Sammamish River, and pass the entrance to Sammamish River Park. At the next intersection in 0.2 mile, turn west on West Riverside Drive, signed to Blyth Park. Follow the narrow paved road west, then south, for 0.5 mile to its end in the park.

Sammamish River Park (City of Bothell, King County)

Park Area: 57.7 acres
Access: Land
Facilities: Benches, picnic tables, multi-use trail, fitness course stations

Sammamish River Park is some wetland and a parking lot that provides access to the portion of the Sammamish River Trail running through Bothell's city limits. The large gravel lot is located on the west side of 102nd Street on the Sammamish River's south side, just south of the heart of

Bothell. Note that 102nd cannot be reached directly from Bothell Way (Highway 522), but requires a two-block detour northeast onto Main Street.

From the parking lot the paved trail follows the high south bank of the placid river between Bothell Landing Park and Brackett's Landing Park. En route it passes a few picnic tables and benches on riverside plots. "Wildlife" here is a large number of domestic chickens gone wild that hobnob with the mallards. Signs warn against harassing them and other wild animals. A large trailer court on the river's north side east of Bothell has several shoreside mobile homes with porches lining the riverbank—a few

Domestic chickens gone wild populate Sammamish River Park.

even have boat docks. Two boat ramps there are for the use of residents.

Fitness course stations strung along the trail at regular intervals are shaded by tall alder, poplar, or willow. Roughly ¹/₂ mile to the west the riverside trail again crosses to the Sammamish River's north side at a small gravel parking lot a couple blocks west of Northeast 174th Street.

Brackett's Landing (City of Bothell)
Park Area: 0.5 acre
Access: Land, water
Facilities: Picnic tables, bench

George Brackett, one of the region's early pioneers, purchased over 200 acres of prime timberland along the Sammamish River in 1882. Trees Brackett logged from here over the years might have ended up in San Francisco, or perhaps even the Orient. The small riverfront community at the edge of his property became known as Brackett's Landing and is still called that today.

The city of Bothell has created a small park at the entrance to Brackett's Landing, off Highway 522, about ¹/₂ mile east of Bothell. A timber staircase leads from the intersection of Woodinville Drive and Northeast 174th Street down through a narrow V-shaped strip of shaded grass to a low bank at river's edge. Parking is almost nonexistent in the vicinity and, although the shore permits easy landing of watercraft, the only facilities are a couple of picnic tables and a bench sitting above the beach.

Kayaking in the Sammamish River near Bothell

Wilmot Gateway Park (City of Woodinville)

Access: Land
Facilities: (Future) picnic pavilion, picnic tables, rest rooms

This site on the west side of 131st Avenue NE, 0.3 mile south of the heart of Woodinville, is scheduled to become a beautifully landscaped showcase park along the Sammamish River. Park plans call for the lot to be replaced by a long trellised picnic pavilion overlooking a wide lawn. Gazebos in the center and at either end of the covered structure will enhance its "gateway" appearance. Parking will be along the park's east side.

As of 1997 the property held only a large gravel parking lot fronting a riverside fence—the start or end point for many bicycle adventures along the Sammamish River Trail.

Woodin Creek Park (City of Woodinville)

Park Area: 4.1 acres
Access: Land
Facilities: Picnic shelter, picnic tables, benches, tennis court, multipurpose court, horseshoe pits, adjacent trail

A former King County park lying next to the Sammamish River Trail has been converted to a modest Woodinville city park. The small mowed meadow has a parking lot off 131st Avenue NE about 0.25 mile south of the heart of Woodinville. Between the lot and the river are a single-hoop basketball court, a tennis court, horseshoe pits, and a picnic shelter. There is easy access to the riverfront trail for hiking, jogging, or bicycling.

Sixty Acres Park (King County)

Park Area: 60 acres
Access: Land
Facilities: Picnic tables, soccer fields (leased), large general-use field, rest rooms

Winnie the Pooh had his Hundred Acre Wood, but people along the Sammamish River have their Sixty Acres Park. It might not be home to Piglet and Eeyore and their friends, but it certainly does attract youngsters. A pair of huge open grass fields, bisected by Northeast 116th Street, along the Sammamish River's east side are used by soccer-ball-kicking, rocket-firing, and kite-flying throngs. The park's north section has been leased to a youth soccer association that manages more than a dozen soccer fields on the grass expanse. Two sides of the soccer area are flanked by large parking lots; rest rooms are at the northwest corner, near the Sammamish River Trail.

The park's undeveloped portion south of 116th is a mowed grass field, ideal for flying model airplanes and firing model rockets or whatever recreation takes a lot of open space. A large informal parking area at the northwest corner of this section next to 116th gives ready access to the grass fields.

The Sammamish River Trail, separated from the fields by a row of Lombardy poplars, runs along the park's west side for nearly 1/2 mile. Rustic picnic tables at two spots adjacent to the trail overlook the river. The next trail access point to the north is at Northeast 124th Street, 0.3 mile away. Aside from its intersection with the Puget Power Trail, the next access to the south is at Redmond City Hall, 1.7 miles away.

Riverwalk Trail (City of Redmond)

Park Area: 42 acres
Access: Land, water
Facilities: (Future) amphitheaters, benches, fishing pier, floating dock, walkways, public art

This proposal, still in the planning stages as of 1998, will enhance the existing Sammamish River Trail through the heart of Redmond and add new features along the riverbank between Northeast 90th Street and Leary Way NE. The master plan calls for a trail gateway at Northeast 90th, shoreline and wetland habitat enhancements along the river's west side,

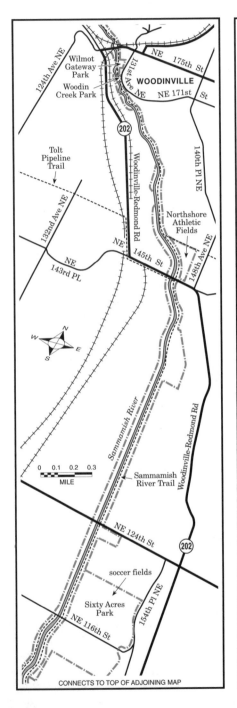

landscaping improvements for the city's municipal campus, and a fishing pier, dock, and trailheads at Northeast 83rd Street. Improvements to Luke McRedmond Park are also planned.

Municipal Campus (City of Redmond)
Park Area: 11 acres
Access: Land
Facilities: Picnic tables, benches, children's play equipment; **(at senior center)** rest rooms, shuffleboard court, pickleball court, boccie ball court, horseshoe pits, picnic tables, public art

This pretty park nicely complements the city-sponsored Redmond Senior Center, which adjoins it. Picnic tables, horseshoe pits, and pickleball, shuffleboard, and boccie ball courts appeal to oldsters, but everyone is welcome to use them. The Redmond City Hall sits north of Northeast 85th Street $1/2$ block east of the Sammamish River. The two-block-long grass terrace between the city hall and the river has several large abstract art works, a children's play area, and more picnic tables and benches. The senior center, north of the municipal building, also fronts on the riverside lawn. Rest rooms there are open to the public during daylight hours.

Stairs on the south side of the Northeast 85th Street bridge lead down to both banks of the river; the low bank offers an easy spot to drop in paddlecraft. Parking lots at the municipal building are open to Sammamish River Trail users for parking on weekends.

Luke McRedmond Park (City of Redmond)
Park Area: 2.11 acres
Facilities: Benches, picnic tables, picnic shelter, small boat landing, information kiosk, public art

This pleasant grass bowl on the Sammamish River's east bank lies in the heart of Redmond, just south of Northeast Redmond Way. Its water fountain and picnic tables make it a popular wayside along the Sammamish River Trail; nearby stores provide vittles for hikers and bikers. A concrete ramp angles down the bank to a low deck at river's edge. Low stairs leading into the water facilitate launching and retrieval of hand-carried boats. A small shelf on the river's opposite west bank has a pair of picnic tables nestled beneath the draping branches of a large willow tree.

At the park's southwest corner, a kiosk offers all sorts of useful information: park maps, local history, nearby services, and a discussion of wildlife management in the park. (Basically, don't feed the waterfowl to avoid being ankle deep in goose poop.) Hoped-for future improvements to the park include rest rooms, a salmon pool and wetlands, and play areas.

Sammamish Slough Park House (King County)

Park Area: 1.67 acres
Access: Land
Facilities: Caretaker's house, Native American cultural center, carving demonstration sheds, plant trail, public art

Adjacent to the Sammamish River Trail at Leary Way, the Sammamish Slough Park House sits on a block of county park property purchased as a part of the trail acquisition. It served as home for artist-in-residence W. C. Carter, a Native American wood-carver whose massive works are still displayed on the premises. When Carter died in 1992 at the age of 101, friends and former apprentices lobbied to have the house and adjoining park remain a memorial to him, offering cultural and arts programs on Native American carving, art classes, public events, seminars, and a continuing artist-in-residence program. The park's fate is uncertain as of 1998, but for the time being, you can tour the tiny grounds from 10:00 A.M. to 4:00 P.M. Tuesday through Thursday, and Saturday and Sunday. Offer your opinion on the property's future in a questionnaire available at a kiosk near the entrance.

Town Center

This former 44-acre golf course along the banks of Bear Creek and the Sammamish River was converted in 1997 to a complex of office buildings, apartments, hotels, and retail shops. As a part of the development a wide buffer of public-access open space was left between the complex and the creek and river. These mini-meadows, bordered with trees and plantings, contain several artificial ponds that drain through a cascading set of weirs into the Sammamish River. Trails through this buffer zone wander along the creek and the river; other paths connect to the Sammamish River Trail.

Marymoor Park (King County)

Park Area: 560.92 acres
Access: Land
Facilities: Sports fields (some lighted), tennis courts, equestrian trails, climbing rock, off-leash dog area, velodrome, event hall, parcourse, motorized airfield, children's play equipment, picnic tables, picnic shelters (reservable), benches, wetlands trail, historical museum, archeological site, rest rooms

As with a number of the large fine parks around the area, Marymoor was the estate of a wealthy businessman. James Clise purchased 78 acres of land here in 1904 to build a hunting lodge. He soon added to his land holdings and improved the property until the modest retreat became Willowmoor Farm, a showcase sporting a 28-room mansion, beautifully

landscaped grounds, and open
meadows where prize-winning
Ayshire cattle and championship
Morgan horses were raised. Clise
sold the farm in 1917, and subse-
quent owners, one of whom renamed it Marymoor, operated a
dairy farm here. In 1963 the property was purchased by King County
for a park.

The area on the park's west side,
south of the road, held the landscaped lawns of the estate. The Clise
Mansion, which stands in its center, now houses the Marymoor Historical Museum. Other buildings
contain the park office (stop here

A wetlands frog at Marymoor Park

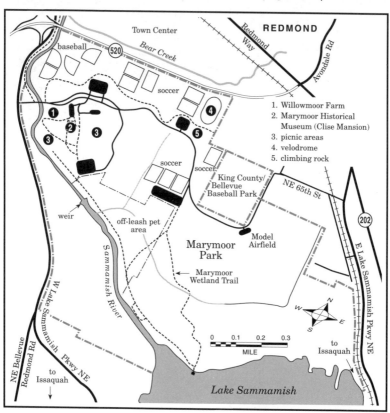

1. Willowmoor Farm
2. Marymoor Historical
   Museum (Clise Mansion)
3. picnic areas
4. velodrome
5. climbing rock

Marymoor Wetland Trail

for a park map and brochures about its features), rest rooms, maintenance buildings, and an art studio. Picnic tables and shelters are nearby. Nearly two dozen unique trees that were planted during the Willowmoor era can be seen as you stroll about the grounds; a park leaflet describes them.

Even considering its large size, it's hard to believe the diverse activities that are packed into the park. Meadows on the north side hold a parcourse, acres of baseball diamonds (some lighted), soccer fields, and tennis courts. A world-class velodrome at the park's northwest end was built for the 1990 Goodwill Games. Adjacent to it are rock-studded concrete slabs of a 45-foot-high practice climbing rock—one of the tallest freestanding practice rocks in the country. Additional huge grass fields, these east of the Clise Mansion, are used for events such as equestrian shows, livestock exhibits, and folk festivals (and more soccer). A nearby miniature airstrip provides space where both radio-controlled and control-line model planes can be flown. An equestrian trail that follows the west side of the river links to Bridle Trails State Park.

The park's south portion is undeveloped. A portion of it is enclosed as an (experimental) off-leash dog exercise area. The remainder of the south end is a wildlife preserve circled by the Marymoor Wetland Trail. Numbered stations along the trail correspond to brochure descriptions of the environment. The trail offers a living portrayal of the succession of habitats from the water lilies, cattails, reed canary grass, and other species of wetland marshes, through low brush, such as Nootka rose, to hardhack and willow that march inland to invade open meadows. A boardwalk floating on peat beds winds through the marsh and reaches a viewing platform overlooking the lake and the Sammamish River entrance. Here in the shallow, lily pad–choked water you might spot fingerling fish, salamanders, tadpoles, and frogs.

It is not possible to launch a hand-carried boat within Marymoor Park; the nearest spot to put in is 0.5 mile to the south at Idylwood Park. That is a fine place to begin a paddle tour of the river. A shallow weir on the west side of Marymoor Park has only enough clearance for paddlecraft; the only other hazard on the river is being beaned by a tossed doggie ball or getting towed ashore by an overeager retriever when abeam of the off-leash area.

To reach the park, take Highway 520 east to the exit of either West Lake Sammamish Parkway NE or East Lake Sammamish Parkway NE, both of which edge the park. The route from the exits to the park is clearly signed.

A windmill along the Sammamish River is a relic from the historic Willowmoor Farm.

Mallards take flight.

LAKE SAMMAMISH

Lake Sammamish meanders north to south for 8 miles along the Cascade foothills. Here is prime boating for whatever you choose—powerboat, sailboat, PWC, inflatable, canoe, or kayak. The long, meandering lake, which is 1 1/2 miles wide throughout most of its length, has plenty of room for everybody. Open water is great for speedboats and water-skiers, shallow water in quiet corners and inlets offers protected water for paddlers. Most of the shore is heavily residential, with just a few public accesses at

selected sites. The entire south end is filled by the very popular Lake Sammamish State Park.

The lake offers excellent fishing for a wide variety of game fish, including largemouth and smallmouth bass, yellow perch, catfish, rainbow trout, cutthroat, kokanee, salmon, and steelhead. Shores along the east and west side drop off quickly to depths of up to 100 feet. Marshy shallows at the north end offer good bass fishing, as do old pilings and submerged trees at the south end in the vicinity of the state park. A salmon hatchery is on the lake's major inlet, Issaquah Creek; water within 1/4 mile of the creek's mouth is closed to salmon fishing.

Idylwood Park (City of Redmond)

Park Area: 17.5 acres
Access: Land, water
Facilities: Picnic tables, dock, swimming beach (guarded in summer), rest rooms

Idylwood Park, the only public beach on the northwest side of Lake Sammamish, is split by Idylwood Creek. The park's north side is a 400-yard deep, gradually sloping, open grass field, tree-lined along the shore. Small powerboats can be drawn up on the beach, and hand-carried boats are easily launched and retrieved here (wheels simplify bringing heavy boats down the long path from the parking lot to the beach). Picnic sites shaded by several large old trees sit on the broad lawn south of the creek. Below is a wide sand beach, edged on the north by a dock. Floats from the dock's end outline the swimming beach.

Tadpoles collect in shallow water of Lake Sammamish.

A paved parking lot is found at the park's northeast corner at the inter-section of Northeast 38th Street and West Lake Sammamish Parkway NE, at the head of the grass field; a concrete path diagonals down from there to the swimming beach. A second gravel path leads down the park's north side to the hand-launch boat area. Crowds drawn to the park on summer weekends rapidly exceed the capacity of the paved lot, but there are two unimproved parking areas on the parkway's west side. A small one is at the triangular intersection of Northeast 36th Street and West Lake Sam-mamish Parkway, and a larger one is on the east side of 177th Avenue NE about a block south of the parkway.

Note that there is a private residence in the center of the park along the parkway's east side. Don't park here or obstruct the drive, or you will be towed.

Timberlake Park (King County)

Park Area: 25 acres
Access: Land, water
Facilities: Swimming beach, picnic tables, 1.2 miles of trail

For those willing to hike the road, this hideaway is an ideal spot for secluded picnicking or swimming. The only land access to the park is a small, easily missed parking lot at the intersection of 184th Avenue SE and Lake Sammamish Parkway SE. The park's narrow strip of woodland stretches between the beach to the road. A gated fire road wends down-hill through open second-growth cedar and hemlock with a fern under-story. As the route approaches the beach, it passes several small open pockets of grass with weathered benches. Concrete pads in one once held a picnic table and barbecue—alas, no longer there. The road ends in a turnaround loop just above the beach where a pair of picnic tables still sit. The pleasant sandy beach fronts a small north-facing cove on the south-west shore of the lake. The park can be recognized from the water by a line of rotted pilings located about 200 yards offshore.

From the water, the beach is an excellent spot to beach a boat for a brief shoreside respite. If King County Parks would put in a sani-can, it would be a terrific spot.

Sammamish Cove Park (King County)

Park Area: 38 acres
Access: Land, water

This undeveloped meadow and wetland along the west side of Lake Sammamish State Park is more a park for fish, amphibians, birds, and mammals that flourish in the wetland environment than for people as there are no recreational improvements. Walk through the thick, high grass for birdwatching, paddle along the shoreline marshlands in a canoe or kayak to observe birds and wildlife, or drop a line in from a boat to catch some of the prize bass that hang out here.

Lake Sammamish State Park (State of Washington)

Park Area: 509 acres
Access: Land, water
Facilities: (State park) picnic tables, picnic shelters (three reservable), barbecues, kitchens, group day-use areas, concession stand, sports field, volleyball courts, swimming beaches (unguarded), bathhouses with showers, kayak rentals (in summer), jogging trail, children's play equipment, horseshoe pits, boat launch ramps (fee), boarding floats, trailer dump station, rest rooms; **(youth group camp)** primitive campsites, picnic shelter, vault toilets

With two beautiful beaches, the only public launch ramp on the lake, and over 6,800 feet of shoreline, this dandy state park along Lake Sammamish's south end draws more than 1.5 million visitors annually. The park's reservable picnic shelters are ideal for company gatherings and family get-togethers; summer weekend dates for these shelters are generally spoken for by early spring.

When the park was built, tons of sand and gravel were dumped on the boggy shore to create the finest freshwater beaches in the region. Most of the activity centers on these swim areas, at the park's southwest corner between Issaquah Creek and the highway. Here, deep green lawns studded with picnic tables are edged with tall old poplar, locust, cedar, and

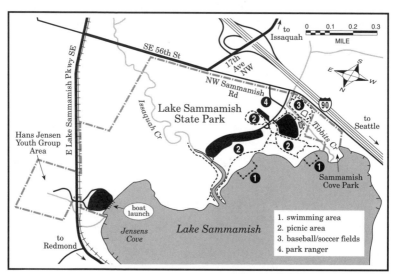

Shelters at Lake Sammamish State Park are often used for family get-togethers.

Douglas-fir. Picnic shelters are distributed far enough apart so the Smith reunion doesn't get mixed in with the Jones reunion. The largest shelter is the Rotunda, a hexagonal-roofed structure between the two beach areas. A large mowed field next to Northwest Sammamish Road has a softball diamond and soccer field and a primitive jogging trail that loops around the perimeter. Bathhouses with summertime concession stands are found at both swimming beach areas; a kayak-rental concession operates out of the east beach bathhouse.

Although crowds of tan-seeking swimmers and sunbathers line the shore on summer weekends, and the boat launch parking lot is crammed with cars and trailers, much of the park's 509 acres along its east side are marshlands and untamed meadows that rarely see human intrusion. Wetlands hold dense growths of cattails, willows, wild iris, and reed canary grass, while the broad meadow is thick with pasture grass, thistles, and head-high snarls of blackberry bushes. A few primitive trails skirt the perimeter of this area or probe tentatively into its edges.

To reach the main park entrance, take Exit 15 (Highway 900W, Renton, Lake Sammamish State Park) from I-90. From the freeway's northeast side, continue east for one block on 17th Avenue NW to the intersection with Northwest Sammamish Road (to the west) and Southeast 56th Street (to the east). Turn west here to reach the beach area in 0.4 mile.

To find the separate boat launch area and the Hans Jensen Youth Group Area, at the above intersection, turn east on Southeast 56th Street. In 0.7 mile go north on East Lake Sammamish Parkway SE. In 1 mile reach the boat launch (on the road's southwest side) and the youth group area (on the road's northeast side). The youth group area, available by reservation only, occupies a narrow meadow flanked by woods. A gravel road, with primitive tent sites and vault toilets scattered along its sides, leads to a picnic shelter and campfire circle.

The nine-lane launch ramp provides a separate tie-down area above the retrieval lanes; parking is between the ramps and the entrance. Canoes and kayaks can be put in here next to the swim beach in the main part of the park, although the latter put-in requires a rather long carry from the parking area. From here you can paddle around the lake edge, or try a more intimate run up Issaquah Creek for a mile or two. Blackberries overhang the stream and beavers or muskrats might be seen. If paddling in Lake Sammamish, watch out for fast-moving boats and water-skiers.

East Lake Sammamish Waterfront Park

(City of Redmond)
Park Area: 3 acres
Access: Land, water
Facilities: (Present) dock with diving board; **(future)** picnic shelter, rest rooms, swimming beach, children's play equipment

This small stretch of beach on the northeast side of Lake Sammamish has been acquired by the city of Redmond, which plans to develop it as a day-use park with picnic facilities and a swimming beach when funds are available. For now, the waterfront is a thick tangle of blackberries and shoreline marsh grasses. An unmarked dirt path leads from East Lake Sammamish Parkway NE to an old dock at the beach with a diving board. As of 1998 there are no signs identifying the property. Look for a gravel pull-off on the parkway's west side opposite the 4300 block of East Lake Sammamish Parkway NE; the path to the beach is below. Until park development occurs, the property is open to the public—but use it at your own risk.

Lake Sammamish Rail-Trail

Length: 12 miles
Access: Land

This hoped-for waterfront trail of the future is, as of 1998, the subject of bitter controversy. Burlington Northern stopped operating trains along the track in the fall of 1996. Although many adjacent landowners

If completed, the Lake Sammamish Rail-Trail would connect with the Sammamish River Trail, shown here, making a 40-mile-long continuous route from Seattle's Shilshole Bay to Issaquah.

support the trail, several very vocal property owners along the old line strongly oppose it and have brought suit to prevent the rail line being used for a trail. Some have erected fences across the property and piled obstacles on the roadbed to prevent its use. Until the legal skirmishes are resolved, public use of the old railbed is questionable and might expose you to retaliation from a few very hostile neighbors.

The conversion of the railroad bed to an extension of the Sammamish River Trail was strongly supported by the Issaquah City Council and the King County Council, and the latter approved funds in the 1997 county budget to purchase the property. The Land Conservancy of Seattle and King County has attempted to purchase the property and hold it until the county can acquire it.

Appendices

A. Emergency Phone numbers and List of Contacts

All western Washington cities and counties use 911 as an emergency number. The following phone numbers are listed as additional contacts for *nonemergency* situations.

Police

King County: (Seattle) (206) 296-3311 or 1-800-344-4080

King County Marine Patrol: King County Courthouse, Seattle, WA 98104. Phone: (206) 296-7559; fax: (206) 205-5371

Kirkland: (425) 828-1183

Mercer Island Marine Patrol: 9611 SE 36th, Mercer Island, WA 98040. Phone: (206) 236-3500

Seattle

Seattle Police Harbor Patrol: 1717 N Northlake Place, Seattle, WA 98103. Phone: (206) 684-4071

U.S. Coast Guard: Pier 36, Seattle, WA 98104. Phone: (206) 442-5295; cell phone: *CG

Radio Contacts
Marine VHF

Coast Guard distress or hailing—Channel 16

Coast Guard liaison—Channel 22

Coast Guard Vessel Tracking Center—Channel 14 (1 watt only)

Hiram M. Chittenden Locks—Channel 13 (1 watt only)

Marine Telephone Service, Seattle—Channels 25 and 26

NOAA Weather Service—Channel WX1

Seattle Ship Canal Bridges—Channel 13 (1 watt only)

OTHER CONTACTS

Hiram M. Chittenden Locks: 3015 NW 54th Street, Seattle, WA 98107. Phone: (206) 783-7000. Internet: http://www.nps.usace.army.mil/opdiv/lwsc/lakewsc.htm

Washington State Department of Natural Resources, South Puget Sound. Regional Office: 950 Farman Street N, P.O. Box 68, Enumclaw, WA 98022-0068. Phone: (360) 825-1631

PARKS

General information regarding state parks is available from Washington State Parks and Recreation Commission, 7150 Cleanwater Lane, Olympia, WA 98504. Internet: http://www.parks.wa.gov. Other information is available from the following organizations:

Bellevue Parks and Recreation: 13204 SE 8th, Bellevue, WA 98009. Phone: (425) 455-6881

Bothell Parks Department: 18305 101st NE, Bothell, WA 98011. Phone: (425) 486-3256

Enatai Beach Park Klub Kayak: Phone (425) 637-8838 or toll free 1-888-765-2925

King County Parks and Recreation Division: 2040 84th SE, Mercer Island, WA 98040. Phone: (206) 296-4232. Internet: http://www.metrokc.gov/parks

Kirkland Department of Parks and Community Services: 123 5th Avenue, Kirkland, WA 98033-6189. Phone: (425) 828-1217

Lake Sammamish State Park: 20606 SE 56th Street, Issaquah, WA 98027. Phone (425) 455-7010

Medina, City Hall: 501 Evergreen Point Road, Medina, WA 98039. Phone: (425) 545-9222

Mercer Island Parks and Recreation: 8236 SE 24th, Mercer Island, WA 98040. Phone: (206) 236-3545

Museum of History and Industry: 2700 24th Avenue East, Seattle, WA 98112-2099. Phone: (206) 324-1126. Internet: http://www.historymuse-nw.org

Redmond Parks and Recreation Department: 15670 NE 85th, Redmond, WA 98052. Phone: (425) 556-2350

Renton Parks and Recreation: 200 Mill Avenue S, Renton, WA 98055. Phone: (425) 235-2568

St. Edward State Park: Box 602, Kenmore, WA 98028. Phone: (425) 823-2992

Seattle Parks and Recreation Department: 600 4th Avenue, Seattle, WA 98104. Phone: (206) 684-4075. Mount Baker Rowing and Sailing Center: 3800 Lake Washington Boulevard S. Phone: (206) 386-1913. Picnic shelter reservations: Phone (206) 684-4081. Washington Park Arboretum Visitor Center: Phone: (206) 543-8800

Woodinville Parks and Recreation: 13203 NE 175th Street, Woodinville, WA 98072. Phone: (425) 489-2700

B. Nautical Charts and Maps

Nautical Chart 690-SC: Lake Washington Ship Canal and Lake Washington. Scale 1:10,000 and 1:25,000.

The Thomas Guide: King County Street Guide and Directory

USGS 7^{1}/$_{2}$ minute quadrangles, (1:24,000 and 1:25,000): Bellevue North, Bellevue South, Edmonds East, Redmond, Renton, Seattle North, Seattle South

C. Selected References

Buerge, David. *Seattle in the 1880s*. Seattle, Washington: The Historical Society of Seattle and King County, 1986.

Churney, Marie, and Susan Williams. *Bogs, Meadows, Marshes and Swamps*. Seattle, Washington: The Mountaineers Books, 1996.

Dorpat, Paul. *Seattle Now and Then*. Seattle, Washington: Paul Dorpat, 1984.

Ficken, Robert E., and Charles P. LeWarne. *Washington: A Centennial History*. Seattle, Washington: University of Washington Press, 1988.

Fisher, Chris C. *Birds of Seattle and Puget Sound*. Redmond, Washington: Lone Pine Publishing, 1996.

Higman, Harry W. and Earl J. Larrison. *Union Bay, the Life of a City Marsh*. Seattle, Washington: University of Washington Press, 1951.

Hunn, Eugene S. *Birding in Seattle and King County*. Seattle, Washington: Seattle Audubon Society, 1982.

Jones, Stan. *Washington State Fishing Guide*. 7th ed. Seattle, Washington: Stan Jones Publishing, Inc., 1995.

Kirk, Ruth, and Carmella Alexander. *Exploring Washington's Past: A Road Guide to History*. Seattle, Washington: University of Washington Press, 1990.

Manning, Harvey, and Penny Manning. *Walks and Hikes in the Foothills and Lowlands around Puget Sound*. Seattle, Washington: The Mountaineers Books, 1995.

McDonald, Cathy M. and Stephen Whitney. *Nature Walks In & Around Seattle*. 2d ed. Seattle, Washington: The Mountaineers Books, 1997.

Wahl, Terence R. and Dennis R. Paulson. *A Guide to Bird Finding in Washington*. rev. ed. Bellingham, Washington: T. R. Wahl, 1986.

Way, Nancy. *Our Town, Redmond*. Redmond, Washington: Marymoor Museum, 1989.

Willingham, William F. *Northwest Passages: A History of the Seattle District U.S. Army Corps of Engineers, 1896–1920*. Seattle District Corps of Engineers, 1992.

D. Quick Reference to Facilities and Recreation

Some types of water recreation, such as boating, paddling, and fishing, are found throughout Seattle's lakes, bays, and waterways. Others, however, are more specific to a particular area. The following table provides a quick reference to the facilities and activities in the major areas covered by this book.

- Moorage/anchorage refers to docks that have guest moorage as well as areas where offshore anchoring is permitted.
- Trailered boat launch refers to hard-surfaced ramps where trailered boats can be launched.
- Hand-carried boat launch refers to both developed launch areas and other points where it is feasible to put in hand-carried craft. Where they impinge on designated swimming areas, some of these may have seasonal restrictions.
- Docks/floats indicates docks, floats, or piers that can be used for temporary moorage, fishing, or swimming, but overnight tie-ups are not permitted.
- Restaurant/fast food generally includes groceries, cafes or restaurants, and fast-food concessions.
- Point of Interest includes historical or educational displays, museums, and self-guided nature trails.

Some facilities listed may be entirely at commercial marinas; some may close off-season. For detailed information read the description of a specific area in the text.

(•) = Nearby

1. THE LOCKS TO LAKE WASHINGTON (pages 27 through 73)

	Paddlecraft Rentals	Boat Rentals	Moorage/Anchorage	Trailered Boat Launch	Hand-Carried Boat Launch	Docks and Floats	Fishing Pier	Paddling	Swimming/Wading	Bicycling	Walking/Hiking	Nature Study	Point of Interest	Restaurants/Fast Food	Picnicking	Sports Fields/Play Equip.	Restrooms/Sani-Cans
Hiram M. Chittenden Locks												•	•	(•)	•		•
24th Avenue NW Park	•	•												(•)			
Fishermen's Terminal													•	•			•
15th Avenue NW Street End					•			•							(•)		
14th Avenue NW Public Boat Launch			•	•	•			•									•
Burke-Gilman Trail: Ballard to the UW										•	•				(•)		(•)
Fremont Canal Park											•	•					

	Paddlecraft Rentals	Boat Rentals	Moorage/Anchorage	Trailered Boat Launch	Hand-Carried Boat Launch	Docks and Floats	Fishing Pier	Paddling	Swimming/Wading	Bicycling	Walking/Hiking	Nature Study	Point of Interest	Restaurants/Fast Food	Picnicking	Sports Fields/Play Equip.	Restrooms/Sani-Cans
South Ship Canal Path										•	•				•		
Etruria Street End										•	•				•		
Cremona Street End										•	•				•		
West Bertona Street End										•	•				•		
Ewing Street Minipark										•	•				•		
6th Avenue West Street End					•			•									
28th Avenue NW					•			•									
11th Avenue NW					•			•									
Gas Works Park										•	•		•	•	•	•	•
Waterway No. 19 Habitat Project					•			•				•					
Sunnyside Avenue Launch Ramp			•	•	•	•		•						(•)			•
Thalilali Park					•							•	•	(•)	•		
North Passage Point Park					•			•						(•)	•		
George Y. Pocock Rowing Center					•	•		•									
South Passage Point Park					•			•							•		
Good Turn Minipark					•			•							•		
Fairview-Olmsted Park					•	•		•				•			•		
East Hamlin Street Minipark					•			•	•						•		
East Roanoke Street Minipark						•		•						(•)	•		
Waterway No. 10 Minipark.					•			•	•					(•)	•		
Waterway No. 8					•	•		•					•				
Terry Pettus Minipark					•	•		•	•						•		
South Lake Union	•	•			•	•		•					•	•	•	•	•
Yale Avenue North Access					•	•								(•)			
Yale Street Landing, Chandler's Cove						•		•					•	•	•	•	•
Maritime Historical Museum													•	(•)			
The Wooden Boat Center.	•							•					•	(•)			•
Northwest Seaport Heritage Center													•				
S Lake Union Park, Waterway No. 3					•			•						(•)	•		

	Paddlecraft Rentals	Boat Rentals	Moorage/Anchorage	Trailered Boat Launch	Hand-Carried Boat Launch	Docks and Floats	Fishing Pier	Paddling	Swimming/Wading	Bicycling	Walking/Hiking	Nature Study	Point of Interest	Restaurants/Fast Food	Picnicking	Sports Fields/Play Equip.	Restrooms/Sani-Cans
East Allison Street End						•		•									
Highland Street						•								(•)			
East Shelby Street						•		•	•								
East Hamlin Street								•	•								
East Edgar Street						•		•	•						•		
Montlake Playfield Park						•		•	•		•	•			•	•	•
West Montlake Park						•		•	•		•				•		
UW: Lower Campus	(•)	•						•		•	•	•	•		•		•
Sakuma Viewpoint	(•)							•							•		
UW Water Activities Center	•	•			•			•		•	•				•		•
Union Bay Marsh								•			•	•	•				
Belvoir Place Minipark					•	•		•							•		
Washington Park Arboretum						•	•	•			•	•	•		•		•
McCurdy Park (MOHAI)											•		•		•		•

2. LAKE WASHINGTON SOUTH (pages 75 through 131)

	Paddlecraft Rentals	Boat Rentals	Moorage/Anchorage	Trailered Boat Launch	Hand-Carried Boat Launch	Docks and Floats	Fishing Pier	Paddling	Swimming/Wading	Bicycling	Walking/Hiking	Nature Study	Point of Interest	Restaurants/Fast Food	Picnicking	Sports Fields/Play Equip.	Restrooms/Sani-Cans
North Madison Park															•	•	
East Madison Street Dock						•	•	•						(•)			
Madison Park									•					(•)	•	•	•
Denny-Blaine Park								•	•						•		
Madrona Park						•			•	•	•			•	•		•
Leschi Park		•				•	•	•	•		•			•	•	•	•
South King Street Minipark											•				•		
South Charles Street End					•				•								
South Norman Street End					•				•								
South Day Street Park					•		•	•	•		•						•
Colman Park							•	•	•	•	•				•		
Mount Baker Park						•			•	•	•		•		•	•	•
Lake Washington Boulevard Park						•				•	•				•		
Stan Sayres Memorial Park	•			•	•	•		•									•

	Paddlecraft Rentals	Boat Rentals	Moorage/Anchorage	Trailered Boat Launch	Hand-Carried Boat Launch	Docks and Floats	Fishing Pier	Paddling	Swimming/Wading	Bicycling	Walking/Hiking	Nature Study	Point of Interest	Restaurants/Fast Food	Picnicking	Sports Fields/Play Equip.	Restrooms/Sani-Cans
Lakewood Moorage			•														
South Ferdinand Street Park					•					•	•						
Seward Park			•				•	•	•	•	•	•	•		•	•	•
Martha Washington Park					•				•		•						
Pritchard Island Beach Park									•						•		•
Beer Sheva Park				•	•	•		•	•						•	•	•
East Lee Street End.					•				•								
East Prospect Street End					•				•								
East Howell Street End									•						•		
60th Avenue SE					•						•						
Calkins Landing									•						•		
Slater Park					•			•	•						•		
Garfield Landing					•			•							•		
Procter Landing					•	•		•	•						•		
Franklin Landing						•		•	•						•		
Miller Landing						•		•	•						•		
Groveland Beach Park						•			•						•	•	•
Clarke Beach Park						•	•	•	•		•				•		•
City Boat Launch				•		•											•
Fruitland Landing					•			•	•						•		
Luther Burbank Park			•			•	•	•	•		•	•	•		•	•	•
Lincoln Landing					•				•						•		
72nd Avenue SE Street End									•						•		
Cedar River Trail					•				•	•	•				•	•	•
Boeing Trail	•	•									•						•
Gene Coulon Memorial Beach Park	•	•	•	•	•	•	•	•	•	•	•	•	•	•	•	•	•
Kennydale Beach Park						•			•						•	•	•
Newcastle Beach Park					•	•		•	•		•	•	•		•	•	•
Southeast 40th Street Boat Launch				•		•											•

	Paddlecraft Rentals	Boat Rentals	Moorage/Anchorage	Trailered Boat Launch	Hand-Carried Boat Launch	Docks and Floats	Fishing Pier	Paddling	Swimming/Wading	Bicycling	Walking/Hiking	Nature Study	Point of Interest	Restaurants/Fast Food	Picnicking	Sports Fields/Play Equip.	Restrooms/Sani-Cans
Mercer Slough Nature Park					•			•		•	•	•	•				•
Enatai Beach Park	•				•	•		•	•						•		•
Chesterfield Beach Park						•		•	•						•		
Burrows Landing Park					•	•		•									
Chism Beach Park					•	•		•	•		•				•	•	•
Meydenbauer Beach Park					•	•		•	•						•	•	•
Clyde Beach Park					•	•		•	•						•	•	•
Medina Beach Park					•	•		•	•						•		•

3. LAKE WASHINGTON NORTH (pages 133 through 165)

	Paddlecraft Rentals	Boat Rentals	Moorage/Anchorage	Trailered Boat Launch	Hand-Carried Boat Launch	Docks and Floats	Fishing Pier	Paddling	Swimming/Wading	Bicycling	Walking/Hiking	Nature Study	Point of Interest	Restaurants/Fast Food	Picnicking	Sports Fields/Play Equip.	Restrooms/Sani-Cans
Burke-Gilman Trail: UW to Kenmore										•	•			(•)	(•)		(•)
Magnuson Park			•	•	•			•	•	•	•	•	•	•	•	•	•
NOAA at Sand Point											•		•	(•)			
Matthews Beach Park								•	•		•				•	•	•
Tracy Owen Station			•	•	•	•		•	•	•	•	•			•		•
St. Edward State Park								•	•	•	•	•	•		•	•	•
Northeast 130th Place Street End				•	•												
O. O. Denny Park					•			•	•		•	•			•		•
Juanita Beach Park					•	•		•	•					(•)	•	•	•
Juanita Bay Park								•				•	•		•		•
Kiwanis Park											•	•					
Waverly Beach Park					•	•	•	•	•						•	•	•
Marina Park		•	•			•			•		•			•	(•)	•		•
Kirkland Yacht Club Marina Dock		•				•								(•)			
Kirkland Shoreline Walkways											•						
David E. Brink Park						•	•	•	•					•		•	
Settlers Landing						•	•				•			(•)			
Marsh Park					•	•	•	•	•							•	•
Houghton Beach Park					•	•	•	•	•					(•)	•	•	•

	Paddlecraft Rentals	Boat Rentals	Moorage/Anchorage	Trailered Boat Launch	Hand-Carried Boat Launch	Docks and Floats	Fishing Pier	Paddling	Swimming/Wading	Bicycling	Walking/Hiking	Nature Study	Point of Interest	Restaurants/Fast Food	Picnicking	Sports Fields/Play Equip.	Restrooms/Sani-Cans
Carillon Point			•			•							•	•			•
Yarrow Bay Wetlands								•				•					
Morningside Park								•				•					
Northeast 47th Street Beach					•			•	•								
Northeast 42nd Street End				•				•									
Fairweather Bay Dock						•											

4. THE SAMMAMISH RIVER AND LAKE SAMMAMISH (pages 167 through 194)

	Paddlecraft Rentals	Boat Rentals	Moorage/Anchorage	Trailered Boat Launch	Hand-Carried Boat Launch	Docks and Floats	Fishing Pier	Paddling	Swimming/Wading	Bicycling	Walking/Hiking	Nature Study	Point of Interest	Restaurants/Fast Food	Picnicking	Sports Fields/Play Equip.	Restrooms/Sani-Cans
68th Avenue NE Launch Ramp			•	•													•
Kenmore Park												•			•	•	•
Swamp Creek Park												•					
Burke-Gilman, Sammamish River Trails								•		•	•	•	(•)	•		(•)	
Bothell Landing Park				•				•		•	•	•		(•)	•	•	•
Blyth Park								•			•	•			•	•	•
Sammamish River Park								•		•	•	•			•		
Brackett's Landing								•							•		
Wilmot Gateway Park								•	•								
Woodin Creek Park								•	•						•	•	
Sixty Acres Park															•	•	•
Riverwalk Trail								•	•				•	(•)	•		
Municipal Campus								•	•				•		•	•	(•)
Luke McRedmond Park				•				•		•	•		•	(•)	•		
Sammamish Slough Park House													•				
Town Center								•	•				•	•			
Marymoor Park								•		•	•	•	•		•	•	•
Idylwood Park				•	•			•	•						•		•
Timberlake Park								•	•			•			•		
Lake Sammamish State Park	•			•	•			•	•	•	•	•			•	•	•
East Lake Sammamish Waterfront Park						•		•	•								

INDEX

Numbered streets are listed at the end of the index.

ABOUT THE AUTHORS

Marge and Ted Mueller are outdoor enthusiasts and environmentalists who have explored Washington State's waterways, mountains, forests, and deserts for nearly 40 years. Ted has taught classes on cruising the Northwest waters, and Marge and Ted have instructed mountain climbing. They are members of The Mountaineers, the Sierra Club, The Nature Conservancy, and the Washington Water Trails Association.

THE MOUNTAINEERS, founded in 1906, is a nonprofit outdoor activity and conservation club, whose mission is "to explore, study, preserve, and enjoy the natural beauty of the outdoors. . . ." Based in Seattle, Washington, the club is now the third-largest such organization in the United States, with 15,000 members and five branches throughout Washington State.

The Mountaineers sponsors both classes and year-round outdoor activities in the Pacific Northwest, which include hiking, mountain climbing, ski-touring, snowshoeing, bicycling, camping, kayaking and canoeing, nature study, sailing, and adventure travel. The club's conservation division supports environmental causes through educational activities, sponsoring legislation, and presenting informational programs. All club activities are led by skilled, experienced volunteers, who are dedicated to promoting safe and responsible enjoyment and preservation of the outdoors.

If you would like to participate in these organized outdoor activities or the club's programs, consider a membership in The Mountaineers. For information and an application, write or call The Mountaineers, Club Headquarters, 300 Third Avenue West, Seattle, Washington 98119; (206) 284-6310.

The Mountaineers Books, an active, nonprofit publishing program of the club, produces guidebooks, instructional texts, historical works, natural history guides, and works on environmental conservation. All books produced by The Mountaineers are aimed at fulfilling the club's mission.

Send or call for our catalog of more than 300 outdoor titles:
The Mountaineers Books
1001 SW Klickitat Way, Suite 201
Seattle, WA 98134
1-800-553-4453
e-mail: mbooks@mountaineers.org
website: www.mountaineers.org